Panini

Gourmet Recipes to Help You Get the Most from Your Panini Press

DOMINIQUE AND CINDY DUBY

DEFINITIVE KITCHEN CLASSICS

whitecap

Edited by Carolyn Stewart
Cover design by Michelle Furbacher & Mauve Pagé
Interior design by Janine Vangool
Typeset by Mauve Pagé
Food styling and photography © 2010
  by Dominique and Cindy Duby

Library and Archives Canada Cataloguing in Publication

Duby, Dominique, 1961–
  Panini : gourmet recipes to help you get the most from your panini press / Dominique & Cindy Duby.

(Definitive kitchen classics)
Includes index.
ISBN 978-1-77050-030-3

  1. Panini. I. Duby, Cindy, 1960– II. Title. III. Series: Definitive kitchen classics

TX818.D82 2011   641.8'4   C2010-904645-5

Printed in China by 1010 Printing Asia Ltd.

The publisher acknowledges the financial support of the Government of Canada through the Canada Book Fund (CBF) and the Province of British Columbia through the Book Publishing Tax Credit.

10 11 12 13 14   5 4 3 2 1

TABLE OF CONTENTS

REPORTS SUGGEST THAT THE FIRST SANDWICH, MADE IN THE FIRST CENTURY BC, WAS A MIXTURE OF CHOPPED NUTS, APPLES, SPICES, AND WINE ENCASED BETWEEN TWO PIECES OF UNLEAVENED BREAD, WHICH WAS EATEN WITH BITTER HERBS. HOW FAR THE SANDWICH HAS COME!

Before the invention of the fork, thick slices of bread, called trenchers (from the French verb *trenchier* or *trancher*, which means "to cut") were an integral part of a table setting. The bread was used to lift cooked food and its sauce from plate to mouth. With the advent of the fork, using fingers to lift food became bad manners and the trencher disappeared. The closest thing to today's sandwich may have come in the late seventh century. While most breads in those days were free-form, the British started to make loaves of white bread in tins, which ensured a uniform shape. Bread made this way also had less crust, so there was more dough to absorb juices and spreads and to hold ingredients together.

The sandwich became very popular in North America during the 1900s when bakeries began to sell presliced bread. The public warmed to its easy preparation, and a food institution was born. Over the years, the sandwich evolved into a variety of specialty items such as the popular panini.

Panini, which originate in Italy, are typically meat and cheese sandwiches that are served hot after being pressed in a grill. The word *panino* is Italian for "small bread roll," and *panino imbottito* ("stuffed panino") refers to the sandwich. The plural of *panino* is *panini* (though outside Italy, *panini* is often used incorrectly as a singular word and pluralized as *paninis*).

Panini are definitely one of our favorite meals, and as with everything we do at our company, we wanted to push the envelope of creativity through the process we call Wild Sweets® FoodArt. Although panino sandwiches are very simple in concept, and the recipes in this book are very easy indeed, we wanted to include new and creative elements. For example, we designed some quick savory (and sweet) dried fruit butters, not only to add unique new flavor profiles and textures but also to act as moisture barriers to keep the bread crisp. We also included some unique panino options made with a raw bread dough that cooks at the same time as the filling in the panini press. Think oven-baked fresh bread, crispy on the outside, with a warm filling inside, and it only takes 4 minutes to bake! Do give the raw-dough panini a try (see pages 56, 64, and 82)—you will be amazed by the texture that results.

And we developed some unique sweet panino recipes based on the same construction principles used for the savory sandwiches. Although most of our sweet panini do include cheese, like their savory counterparts, the bread portion is typically sweet (e.g., croissant, brioche, or even crêpes) and the vegetable or meat fillings are replaced with prepared fruits, as well as luscious creams and smooth butters. A separate chapter includes basic recipes, as well as tips and tricks for quick-cooking techniques and more. Also included is a chapter on pairing beer and wine with panini. We hope our creations will inspire you to add your own flair and invent your very own panino. Keep in mind that panini are easy to make, with countless flavor combinations, sweet and savory. Above all, they are a delicious all-in-one meal.

Panini 101

Panini have all the makings of a great, yet simple, gastronomical delight provided you have a good understanding of the basic ingredients and apply some creative culinary thinking to them. We wanted to look at the architecture of the panino and apply our own Wild Sweets® FoodArt creative design process to it. This process, born of our culinary philosophy of *constructivism*, starts with identifying and defining what each part of the panino brings to the whole, and then constructing from there. In other words, we wanted to know what makes a panino great—what works or does not, and why. Before you begin constructing your own panini, there are some factors you should keep in mind. Here is an at-a-glance list for you to consider:

AUDIENCE: It is important to identify for whom you are making the panini so your panini can meet the needs of that specific audience. For example, are the panini to be served at a children's party, a business lunch, or a casual dinner with close friends? Children typically do not like strong flavors, too many flavors, or even certain textures. Also take into account the thickness of the bread and the size of the panini when cooking for children or business-people, as too large or thick a panino can be difficult to eat. Business functions typically mean business attire, so you should consider that panini made with runny cheeses or sauces or loose ingredients may be prone to leaking.

SERVICE: How many people are coming to your party? Will you have time to stay away from your guests in order to cook? Are you planning to assemble and cook the panini just before serving? Each of these scenarios will require different planning and setup. In any event, we recommend a good *mise en place*, with all ingredients assembled, premeasured, prepared (e.g.,

sliced), and possibly preportioned for each panino. If you do not have much time available, you may want to consider designing panini that can be put together several hours ahead of time and then just need to be grilled. Keep in mind that some fillings and breads will not withstand long storage, and some ingredients will not marry well over time.

DESIGN: After identifying your target audience and service requirements, designing panini becomes a lot easier. In the next paragraphs, you will find specific information pertaining to the main components of panini, which will help in the design process:

- An overly thick or crispy bread will, more often than not, make the filling spill out of the panini. So keep the bread thin if you have a loose filling. The exception would be for moister fillings, where you most likely want the bread, at least the bottom slice, to be slightly thicker so it can absorb the excess moisture when pressed. Overly crispy bread can also make panini hard to eat because it is not easy to bite through and it can scratch the roof of the mouth and the gums.

- Keep in mind that whatever ingredients you select, they are intended to work as a combination of flavors and textures that is consistent in every bite. Therefore it is important, when building your panini, to have all of the ingredients portioned correctly and laid evenly over the surface of the bread. For example, you do not want one or two bites of a panino to have all the cheese and the remaining bites to have all the meat. The same goes for the sauce, condiments, and any other complementary flavor elements you are including in your panini. What's more, an unevenly constructed panino will not grill properly or heat through.

- With moister fillings, consider using a semihard cheese and placing a slice directly on the bottom piece of the bread, so the cheese can act as a moisture barrier and keep the bread from becoming soggy.

- Keep in mind how the taste groupings (sweet—salty—acidic—bitter) relate between the leading and secondary ingredients, so that the overall flavors are all well balanced. For example, it is best not to use two acidic elements, like cornichon pickles and pickled vegetables, together in the same panino. You are better off to have each element bring its own distinct flavor and stand out for it within the panino rather than be masked or overpowered by the others.

INGREDIENTS

THE BREAD: Bread is the predominant ingredient in a panino, and it provides the backbone or main structure. It is commonly agreed that ciabatta is the best bread to make panini, and after many tests in our lab we would have to concur.

Ciabatta is an Italian white bread made with wheat flour and yeast. Ciabatta bread has a crisp crust and a somewhat soft, porous texture, and it is light to the touch. In Italy, ciabatta has either a firm crust and a dense crumb or a crisper crust and more open texture, depending on the region where it is made. We have found that the best type of ciabatta for panini is the more open-crumbed form made from a very wet dough and a *biga* (sourdough starter), which is the style typically available in North America.

Making ciabatta requires machine kneading for the best results, but it can be made fairly easily at home in a stand mixer with a dough hook attachment (see page 128). Alternatively, you may consider using focaccia or a good sourdough bread—even a kaiser roll. We have discovered another, quite unique, bread option, which is to make panini with raw bread dough that is cooked at the same time as the filling in the panini press. This technique, using pizza-type dough, yields a panino that is very similar to a calzone in taste, with a soft crumb and thin crispy crust, a fresh bread taste on the outside, and a warm filling inside that releases its aroma when you bite into it. The recipe for this easy dough can be found in the Basic Recipes section (see page 126).

THE CHEESE: In a panino, the cheese is typically the ingredient that unites the other elements or flavors, while adding its own taste and aroma—from subtle to pungent. As cheese melts, it forms a moisture barrier if placed directly on the bread and helps bind the fillings and the two pieces of bread together. Try to select a cheese that will harmonize with or complement the leading flavors of your panini. The cheese should melt easily, but not be so fatty that it separates and leaks onto the grill or makes the panini gooey. There are many different types of cheese produced throughout the world in a wide range of flavors, textures, forms, and milk sources (usually cow, but also buffalo, goat, and sheep). Cheese styles, textures, and flavors depend on the milk's origin and whether or not it has been pasteurized, the butterfat content, the bacteria and mold, the processing, and the aging. Herbs, spices, or wood smoke may be used as flavoring agents. Here is a list of cheese styles particularly well suited to panini making:

- **BUTTERY CHEESES** are typically mild tasting, without a distinctly pronounced flavor or aroma. Buttery cheeses include Edam, Gouda,

Bel Paese, and Fontina. These cheeses are usually firm, supple, and easily sliced.

- **SWISS-STYLE CHEESES** typically have tough rinds and interiors dotted with holes caused by gas expansion during the ripening period. They usually have a mild, sweetish, nutty flavor. The most common varieties of Swiss-style cheeses include Emmentaler, Gruyère, Sbrinz, and Raclette.

- **CHEDDAR** is one of the most popular and widely copied cheeses in the world. Cheeses that are *cheddared* have been cut into pieces, stacked, and turned inside the cheese vat for a given period of time. The typical cheddar cheese has a firm texture and is yellow in color, with a clean, mellow taste that develops a sharp and tangy bite as it matures. Leading English varieties include Gloucester, Cheshire, Leicester, Lancashire, Derby, Wensleydale, and Stilton, which is considered a blue-veined cheddar. The United States, Australia, Canada, France, and New Zealand also make cheddar cheeses.

- The majority of **HARD CHEESES** are made in the Italian *grana* style. They have a hard, brittle texture, perfect for grating and panini making, and a sharp, piquant flavor. Parmesan is the best-known cheese of this style.

- **MONASTERY CHEESES**, named for their monastic origins, are mostly of the washed-rind variety. Some of the best-known cheeses in the monastery category include Port Salut, Saint Paulin, and Trappist. Havarti, Beaumont, and Reblochon are also classified as monastery-type cheeses.

- **BLUE CHEESES** are characterized by their internally ripened blue, blue-black, or blue-green veining (the result of a *Penicillium* spore inoculation), pungent aromas, and tangy flavors. Typically soft cheeses, they can be crumbly in texture or exceptionally soft—even spreadable. Roquefort, Stilton, and Gorgonzola are considered to be the three best blue-veined cheeses in the world.

- **GOAT CHEESES**, made from goat's milk, are usually quite small and come in a variety of shapes and sizes such as pyramids, cones, and cylinders. Their characteristically goaty flavor, quite subtle to fairly pungent, depends on the length of time the cheese is aged. The word *chèvre* is French for "goat," and the term is used to refer to goat cheese in general.

THE MEAT: The meat in a panino can include cuts prepared in an array of styles, from cured to roasted, braised, dried, cased, confit, corned, or even gelled. As with the cheese, the meat element offers many different flavors and aromas, ranging from subtle to pungent. Different preparation styles can result in very different textures as well, ranging from soft to chewy, and even crispy. When selecting a meat for your panini, keep in mind that it should harmonize with or complement the other flavors. The amount and thickness of the meat are also important. A generous amount of fork-tender pulled pork will easily give way to most jaws, but not so for a large amount of thickly sliced, tougher dried or cured meat. So, make sure that such meat is sliced very thinly.

As with cheeses, there are many different types of prepared meats produced throughout the world in wide-ranging flavors, textures, and forms. Here is a list of meat types that are particularly well suited to panini making (see also pages 117–18 on preparing meats not typically available at grocery store meat counters):

- **CURED MEATS** have been treated with a solution of salt, sugar, spice, and nitrate or nitrite. The salty brine dehydrates the meat while the nitrate converts itself into another form, resulting in a meat with an attractive pink color when cooked. Further processing can include smoking. Probably the most famous cured meat is ham, including Smithfield ham from Virginia and specially cured hams such as prosciutto from Italy, serrano from Spain, and Bayonne from France. Other cured meats include bacon, which is typically smoked (sometimes even double-smoked), with the exception of pancetta and back bacon, which are unsmoked.

- **CORNED MEATS** are also brine-cured, but then cooked. Corned beef is typically a cut of brisket that is cured or pickled in a seasoned brine and then cooked. It is often purchased ready to eat in delicatessens. Pastrami is similar to corned beef, except that the meat has been seasoned with various herbs and spices and then smoked.

- **SALAMI** are cured, fermented, and air-dried sausages. There are many different varieties. Some of the best-known salami from Italy include cacciatore, capocollo, and soppressata. American versions include Genoa salami and pepperoni. French salami include saucisson sec and cervelat.

- **COLD CUTS**, sometimes called luncheon meats, come in many varieties and are typically sold in sausage-shaped logs of different sizes. Some of the most common are American bologna, a smokehouse-cooked, seasoned Italian-style sausage (sometimes also referred to as baloney), and the similar Italian mortadella, with cubes of pork fat studded throughout. Other common cold cuts include bierwurst, a Bavarian-style sausage sometimes called summer sausage, and kielbasa, an Eastern European–style garlic sausage.

- **SAUSAGES**, unlike most salami, are small and typically served whole, cut, or, if cooked out of their casings, crumbled. Sausages can be fresh or dried, and made not only from beef or pork, but also from lamb, chicken, duck, turkey, or even wild game such as venison. Some of the best-known varieties are merguez, bratwurst, chorizo, bangers, chipolata, Cumberland, kielbasa, Linguiça, and andouille.

THE CONDIMENTS: In order to be creative at panini making, as well as at cooking in general, you need a well-stocked pantry. Condiments should bring a distinct layer of flavor that either complements or contrasts with the leading flavors of the panini. For example, on the savory side, the acidity of pickles contrasts with the fattiness of salami or other charcuterie. Rich sauces like mayonnaise contrast with lean cuts of meat. Mustard is quite versatile, as it can bring sweetness as well as acidity. Pickled vegetables add great flavor balance, as well as crisp and/or crunchy textures. Canned bean mash can become one of the leading flavors or it can just add texture. On the sweet side, the richness (and sometimes also the saltiness) of nut butters can balance nicely with sweet or slightly acidic jams, preserves, and marmalades. Dried fruits make fantastic butters that encapsulate flavor in elements both sweet (e.g., saffron) and savory (e.g., balsamic vinegar).

Many condiments are commonly available and can be kept at room temperature in the pantry, though others require refrigeration. For the latter, it is best to buy as little as possible in case they spoil or take on (and disperse) unwanted aromas in your refrigerator. Keep in mind that many condiments can also be made rather than purchased. They do take time to make, but you will end up with preparations that are fresher and have a better texture than their store-bought counterparts. However, that philosophy does not apply to all condiments; for example, you are better off buying sauerkraut than attempting to make your own. See the Basic Recipes chapter (starting on page 115) for our condiment recipes. (Some use store-bought ingredients and are easy to put together.)

To get you started, here is a list of recommended items to keep on hand:

- **FAT:** Extra virgin olive oil; flavored oils such as truffle oil; butter; and high-quality margarine. You will use them for sautéing vegetable fillings and for spreading on the outside of panini before grilling.

- **ACID:** A selection of different vinegars including a well-aged balsamic, as well as character vinegars such as sherry.

- **SALT AND PEPPER:** Sea salt such as Maldon and fleur de sel; smoked salt; and whole peppercorns.

- **SPICES:** As many as you like but especially pungent spices such as curry, ancho chili powder, saffron, *ras el hanout*, aniseed, chilies, and fennel seeds.

- **BEANS:** Canned beans are the quickest to use, but dried beans are a good option, especially for varieties that are not available canned.

- **MUSTARD:** A selection of different styles such as grainy moutarde de Meaux, Dijon, honey, and dried mustard.

- **FISH/SHELLFISH:** Canned fish such as tuna, salmon, mackerel, and anchovies; canned shellfish such as smoked oysters or mussels; and perhaps some pickled fish such as herring.

- **PICKLED ITEMS:** A selection of pickles such as cornichon or gherkin; baby dill; sweet; and bread and butter; as well as pickled banana peppers.

- **BRINED ITEMS:** A good selection of olives (such as black kalamata, niçoise, and green Sicilian), as well as sauerkraut and capers.

GRILLING EQUIPMENT

A panini press is basically a double-sided cooking device that cooks both sides of a sandwich simultaneously, leaving the distinctive grill marks that classic panini are known for. Due to the popularity of panini, there are many brands of grills, and options within each brand, on the market today. So, how to choose? Most panini presses feature grooved top and bottom heated plates, but some manufacturers offer the option of a grooved top plate combined with a flat bottom plate. A grill with the option of a smooth lower surface offers more versatility, as it allows you to cook food items that don't require grill marks, such as eggs and pancakes. Unless you are looking for a heavy-duty commercial unit, most electric panini presses are quite compact and designed to be used on a countertop.

Commercial grills can offer very desirable features not available to the home cook, such as separate temperature controls for the upper and lower plates. Panini presses for home use may offer a fixed heat, or a temperature dial that allows you to set the temperature for both the top and bottom plates, from low to medium to high. More deluxe models even feature an LCD screen for the temperature, the cooking setting, and the timer. If your grill does not include a timer, we strongly suggest that you invest in one. Digital timers are very inexpensive and will pay for themselves in no time—you will no lon-

ger have to risk getting distracted and burning a few panini. Not to mention that exact timing will yield a perfect panino time after time with no guessing, provided the panino is built more or less the same.

The power of the unit or model is another factor to consider. If you are planning to cook only one or two panini at any given time, this might not be a concern. However, if you are planning to cook for a party or larger family, the more power the better. In any event, for good heat retention and recovery time, we recommend units that are at least 1500 watts and preferably 1800 watts. The more wattage a unit has, the faster it will reach its set temperature and regain it after loading and unloading.

You should also think about the grill surfaces and which type will best suit your needs, again in terms of heat retention and recovery time. Materials used to cast panini machine plates include aluminum, iron, and stainless steel, and these can also be nonstick-coated. As a general rule, aluminum heats quickly but loses heat quickly as well. Cast iron takes longer to heat, but retains that heat for a longer time. And stainless steel, the most durable material of the three, heats quickly and also distributes heat efficiently. Some of the grills on the market today offer QuanTanium nonstick surface plates, which are reportedly engineered for extreme durability. In any event, nonstick surface plates, regardless of the plate material, are generally the best option to consider. Nonstick plates are also much easier to clean and are the best choice for those who prefer to cook with little or no fat.

Some of the other features that we like in a panini press include an adjustable grilling-height control, which offers much more versatility when grilling many different types of panini, especially those with softer fillings. The weight of the top plate is often too heavy for grilling panini with soft fillings and can push the filling out of the bread. A grill with adjustable settings allows you to set the top plate at a certain height, which will reduce the amount of pressure applied by the top plate on more delicate panini, and thus prevent the filling from being pressed out of the bread. Another feature we highly recommend is a drip tray. A drip tray is a wonderful little device that is mounted at the front of the machine below the bottom plate, set at an angle for easy flow of fat and other drippings. The drip tray makes the grilling of high-fat foods such as bacon, for example, much easier and cleaner.

If you do not have an electric panini press, another option to consider is a panini pan and press. This nonelectric device consists of a bottom pan, typically nonstick, and a heavy-duty panini press top with a ridged surface and a handle that weighs down the panino. The pan and top must be heated separately using an external source such as the stove elements. Once hot, the process is basically the same as grilling with an electric unit. Note that the material of the panini pan and press is even more important than with an electric grill, as good heat retention is imperative without a built-in heat source.

Grilled Bread & Cheese

Classic Grilled Cheddar Cheese Panini

4 slices white bread

4 oz (120 g) cheddar cheese, sliced

Butter, for spreading

ALTERNATIVES

Bread: *country or sourdough*

Cheese: *Gouda or Jarlsberg*

The classic Grilled Cheese is the basis of just about every composed sandwich. The bread and cheese components can be interchanged in many different flavor combinations. In this chapter, we offer several recipe ideas; you can of course substitute or combine ingredients according to your taste. A basic grilled bread and cheese panino can easily be made using leftovers in your fridge. For example, if you have some roasted potatoes left over, some cream cheese, and perhaps some green onions or chives, you have got yourself a great panino! Make it even more satisfying by adding a few slices of smoked salmon, maybe a few capers, and some sliced onions to your sandwich, and serving it alongside a fresh green salad. Voilà—a great meal in a snap. As far as combinations are concerned, the only limit is your imagination.

Preheat the press to medium (375°F / 190°C).

To build each panino, arrange ingredients in the following order: white bread, cheddar cheese, white bread.

Spread butter on outside of panini (top and bottom) and grill for about 5 to 8 minutes, or until cheese is melted and bread is nicely grilled.

Gruyère, Ciabatta & Onion Jam Panini

4 slices ciabatta bread, or 2 ciabatta buns, halved

4 oz (120 g) Gruyère cheese, sliced

4 Tbsp (60 g) Caramelized Onion Jam (see page 125)

Butter, for spreading

ALTERNATIVES

Bread: country or sourdough

Cheese: Emmentaler or Sbrinz

The sweet and slightly acidic taste and jamlike texture of the caramelized onion work well with the Gruyère in this panino. As an option, you may experiment with store-bought chutney that has the same sweet-acidic taste profile.

Preheat the press to medium (375°F / 190°C).

To build each panino, arrange or spread ingredients in the following order: ciabatta, one-quarter Gruyère, Caramelized Onion Jam, one-quarter Gruyère, ciabatta.

Spread butter on outside of panini (top and bottom) and grill for about 5 to 8 minutes, or until cheese is melted and bread is nicely grilled.

Saint Agur, Raisin Bread & Honey-Nut Panini

4 slices raisin bread

2 oz (60 g) Saint Agur cheese, sliced
or crumbled

20 whole hazelnuts, roasted and crushed

2 tsp (10 g) liquid honey

Butter, for spreading

ALTERNATIVES

Bread: dried fruit such as cranberry or fig

Cheese: Gorgonzola or another blue cheese

The success of this panino lies in the contrast
between the sweet elements and the unique,
somewhat salty flavor of the Saint Agur cheese.
However, any combination of a sweet or fruited
bread with a blue-veined cheese would work
well as an alternative, so feel free to create a new
panino flavor combination.

Preheat the press to medium (375°F / 190°C).

To build each panino, arrange or spread ingredients
in the following order: raisin bread, Saint Agur,
crushed hazelnuts, honey, raisin bread.

Spread butter on outside of panini (top and bottom)
and grill for about 5 to 8 minutes, or until cheese is
melted and bread is nicely grilled.

Chèvre, Brioche & Wilted Leek Panini

4 slices brioche bread, or 2 brioche buns, halved

2 Tbsp (30 g) butter

½ medium leek, (white and light green parts only), thinly sliced

1 Tbsp (15 mL) finely chopped mint (optional)

Salt and pepper, to taste

3 oz (90 g) soft goat cheese

Butter, for spreading

ALTERNATIVES

Bread: challah or milk bread

Cheese: cream cheese or semihard goat

Vegetable: sautéed green onions

The soft texture and slight sweetness of the brioche combine perfectly with the tangy goat cheese and fragrant minted leek. Sautéed green onions and a dab of mint jelly could work as an alternative.

Preheat the press to medium (375°F/190°C).

Melt 2 Tbsp (30 g) butter in a saucepan on high heat, then add leeks and quickly sauté until wilted, about 1 minute. Remove from heat, add mint (if using), and stir until well mixed. Season to taste with salt and pepper.

To build each panino, arrange or spread ingredients in the following order: brioche, one-quarter goat cheese, leek, one-quarter goat cheese, brioche.

Spread butter on outside of panini (top and bottom) and grill for about 5 to 8 minutes, or until cheese is melted and bread is nicely grilled.

Taleggio, Focaccia & Roasted Tomato Panini

4 slices focaccia bread, or 2 focaccia buns, halved

4 oz (120 g) Taleggio cheese, rind removed, sliced

1 recipe Roasted Tomatoes (see page 115)

Butter, for spreading

ALTERNATIVES

Bread: country or sourdough

Cheese: Edam or Gouda

Vegetable: sweet red pepper

This panino unites classic Italian ingredients. It works especially well as it combines the sweetness of the tomatoes with the supple and fruity taste of the Taleggio, which by the way is also considered an excellent dessert cheese. Grilled sweet red peppers with a drizzle of a well-aged balsamic vinegar would be another option.

Preheat the press to medium (375°F/190°C).

To build each panino, arrange ingredients in the following order: focaccia, one-quarter Taleggio, Roasted Tomatoes, one-quarter Taleggio, focaccia.

Spread butter on outside of panini (top and bottom) and grill for about 5 to 8 minutes, or until cheese is melted and bread is nicely grilled.

Fontina, Sourdough & Mushroom Ragout Panini

4 slices sourdough bread

5 large button mushrooms, sliced

1 clove garlic, finely chopped

1 Tbsp (15 mL) vegetable oil

1 tsp (5 mL) hoisin or barbecue sauce

2 Tbsp (30 mL) water or white wine

Salt and pepper, to taste

4 oz (120 g) Fontina cheese, sliced

Butter, for spreading

ALTERNATIVES

Bread: country or ciabatta

Cheese: Gruyère or Bel Paese

Vegetable: caramelized onions

Together, the sourness of the bread, the somewhat sweet and nutty, almost honeyed, flavor of the Fontina, and the earthiness of the mushroom ragout combine to turn these simple ingredients into a boldly flavored panino. Caramelized onions are an option instead of the mushroom ragout.

Preheat the oven to 450°F (230°C).

In a bowl, combine mushrooms; garlic; oil; hoisin or barbecue sauce; water or white wine; and salt and pepper, and toss until well mixed.

Place mushrooms in an ovenproof pan and roast for approximately 20 minutes, stirring occasionally until all the liquid has evaporated. Remove from oven and set aside.

Preheat the press to medium (375°F/190°C).

To build each panino, arrange ingredients in the following order: sourdough bread, one-quarter Fontina, mushroom ragout, one-quarter Fontina, sourdough.

Spread butter on outside of panini (top and bottom) and grill for about 5 to 8 minutes, or until cheese is melted and bread is nicely grilled.

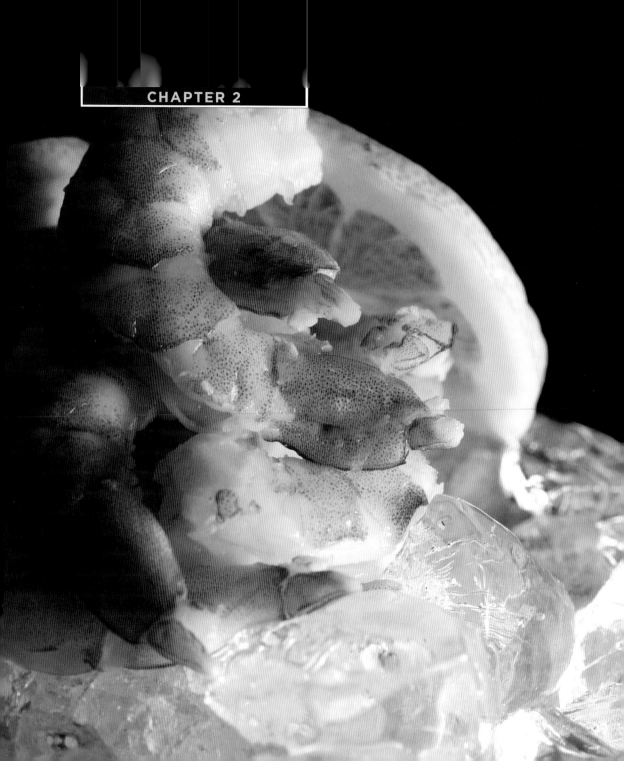

Seafood & Shellfish

Fried Fish, Mashed Peas & Emmentaler Panini

4 slices ciabatta bread, or 2 ciabatta buns, halved

4 small (or 2 large) pieces of frozen fish (any kind), breaded or battered

3 Tbsp (45 g) finely chopped onion

1 clove garlic, finely chopped

3 Tbsp (45 g) butter

1 cup (125 g) frozen peas, thawed and drained

Salt and pepper, to taste

1 Tbsp (15 g) Salsa Verde (see page 122)

¼ cup (60 g) mayonnaise

2 oz (60 g) Emmentaler cheese, sliced

Butter, for spreading

ALTERNATIVES

Bread: country or white

Cheese: Gruyère or Sbrinz

Fish: battered cod or salmon

Garnish: Pesto Sauce (see page 122)

This panino combines some of England's most classic flavors—battered fried fish and mushy peas. This is our quick version of mashed peas with store-bought battered fish. Of course freshly made would be best!

Cook fish according to package instructions. Preheat the press to medium (375°F/190°C).

Prepare mashed peas: sauté onions, garlic, and butter on medium-high heat in a saucepan for 3 minutes or until translucent, then add peas and heat through. Transfer to a food processor, season to taste with salt and pepper, and pulse a few times. Alternatively, mash with a fork. Set aside.

In a small bowl, whisk Salsa Verde and mayonnaise together, and set aside.

To build each panino, arrange ingredients in the following order: ciabatta spread with one-quarter pea mixture, Salsa Verde mayonnaise, fish, Emmentaler, ciabatta spread with one-quarter pea mixture.

Spread butter on outside of panini (top and bottom) and grill for about 5 to 8 minutes, or until cheese is melted and bread is nicely grilled.

Smoked Salmon, Ratatouille & Mozzarella Panini

YIELDS 2 PANINI

4 slices ciabatta bread, or 2 ciabatta buns, halved

½ cup (120 g) Ratatouille (see page 115)

3 oz (90 g) fresh mozzarella cheese, drained and sliced

2 oz (60 g) smoked salmon

Butter, for spreading

ALTERNATIVES

Bread: country or white

Cheese: bocconcini or buffalo mozzarella

Fish: other smoked fish

Garnish: Roasted Tomatoes (see page 115)

Classic French ratatouille is a great dish on its own, and it is even better when combined with the rich and smoky flavor of the salmon and the creamy yet light texture of the fresh mozzarella in this crispy panino.

Preheat the press to medium (375°F / 190°C).

To build each panino, arrange ingredients in the following order: ciabatta spread with one-half ratatouille, mozzarella, smoked salmon, ciabatta.

Spread butter on outside of panini (top and bottom) and grill for about 5 to 8 minutes, or until cheese is melted and bread is nicely grilled.

Olive, Grapefruit & Havarti Tuna Melt Panini

4 slices ciabatta bread, or 2 ciabatta buns, halved

6 oz (170 g) can tuna, drained

16 large green Sicilian olives, pits removed, finely chopped or puréed

3 Tbsp (45 g) Citrus Aioli (made with grapefruit; see page 119)

1 whole grapefruit, segmented

2 oz (60 g) havarti cheese, sliced

4 Tbsp (60 g) Pickled Fennel (see page 116)

Butter, for spreading

ALTERNATIVES

Bread: country or white

Cheese: Comté or manchego

Fish: other canned or cooked fish

Sauce: mayonnaise or tartar

The tuna melt is a great standard, and we think our version will elevate this time-honored sandwich to new heights. Fish and citrus is already a classic flavor combination that when combined with salty-spicy green olives, aromatic grapefruit mayonnaise, and crunchy sweet-acidic Pickled Fennel becomes amazingly irresistible. If you do not have time to make the Pickled Fennel, finely sliced raw sweet onions sprinkled with a few drops of vinegar and a pinch of sugar make a quick alternative, though the flavors are not quite as complex.

Preheat the press to medium (375°F/190°C).

For the tuna filling, combine tuna, olives, and Citrus Aioli in a bowl and mix well with a fork. Slice grapefruit segments ¼ inch (6 mm) thick.

To build each panino, arrange ingredients in the following order: ciabatta spread with one-half tuna mixture, Pickled Fennel, grapefruit, havarti, ciabatta.

Spread butter on the outside of the panini (top and bottom) and grill for about 5 to 8 minutes, or until the cheese is melted and the bread is nicely grilled.

Crab, Mascarpone, Potato Mash & Fresh Herbs Panini

4 slices ciabatta bread, or 2 ciabatta buns, halved

1 medium potato, boiled

1 oz (30 g) mascarpone cheese

2 Tbsp (30 mL) finely chopped fresh herbs (e.g., chives, parsley, tarragon, and chervil)

4 tsp (20 g) horseradish spread

Salt and pepper, to taste

1 cup (100 g) crabmeat, cooked or canned

Butter, for spreading

ALTERNATIVES

Bread: country or white

Cheese: cream cheese or Neufchâtel

Fish: lobster or shrimp

The inspiration for this panino is based on the classic crab cake. The crispy coating is replaced by the grilled bread, which encases a sinfully creamy mascarpone potato filling that is perked up by the freshness of the herbs and the spiciness of the horseradish.

Preheat the press to medium (375°F/190°C).

Mash boiled potato with a fork in a bowl. Add mascarpone and mix to combine. Mix herbs and horseradish in a bowl and season to taste with salt and pepper.

To build each panino, arrange ingredients in the following order: ciabatta spread with one-quarter potato filling, crab, ciabatta spread with horseradish mixture then one-quarter potato filling.

Spread butter on outside of panini (top and bottom) and grill for about 5 to 8 minutes, or until cheese is melted and bread is nicely grilled.

Shrimp Sofrito, Grilled Red Pepper & Manchego Panini

4 slices ciabatta bread, or 2 ciabatta buns, halved

1 large red pepper, halved and seeded

1 tsp (5 mL) olive oil

3 Tbsp (45 g) Caramelized Onion Jam (see page 125)

1 Tbsp (25 g) finely chopped sun-dried tomato

1 clove garlic, finely chopped

¾ cup (100 g) cooked shrimp, coarsely chopped

Salt and pepper, to taste

2 oz (60 g) manchego cheese, rind removed and sliced

Butter, for spreading

ALTERNATIVES

Bread: country or Spanish (pan de horno)

Cheese: feta or pecorino

Fish: crayfish or prawns

Garnish: sautéed onions

Sofrito is a classic Spanish culinary base consisting of slowly cooked onions, garlic, and tomatoes. We use sun-dried tomatoes for a rich tomatoey flavor along with grilled sweet red pepper, finished with the unique sheep-milk manchego cheese for our own version of a classic Spanish-flavored panino.

Preheat the press to medium (375°F/190°C).

Brush both sides of red pepper halves with olive oil and cook in the panini press for about 10 to 12 minutes. Remove peppers and set aside.

Place Caramelized Onion Jam, sun-dried tomato, garlic, and shrimp in a bowl and mix until combined. Season to taste with salt and pepper. Divide shrimp mixture in half and form into 2 patties.

To build each panino, arrange ingredients in the following order: ciabatta spread with roasted red pepper, shrimp patty, manchego cheese, ciabatta.

Spread butter on outside of panini (top and bottom) and grill for about 5 to 8 minutes, or until cheese is melted and bread is nicely grilled.

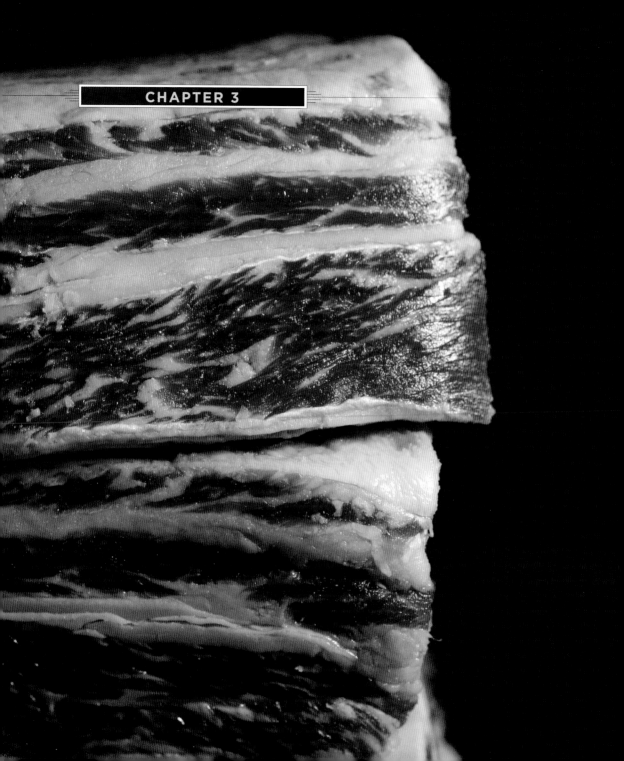

Meat & Poultry

Braised Pork, Date, Wilted Kale & Jack Cheese Panini

4 slices ciabatta bread, or 2 ciabatta buns, halved

1 Tbsp (15 g) butter

4 kale leaves, washed, stems removed

2 Tbsp (30 mL) water

Salt and pepper, to taste

4 Tbsp (60 g) Date Butter (see page 123)

4 oz (120 g) Braised Pork, shredded (see page 118)

1 oz (30 g) Monterey Jack cheese, sliced

Butter, for spreading

ALTERNATIVES

Bread: corn or potato

Cheese: Jarlsberg or provolone

Meat: Chinese-style barbecued pork

Greens: collard or mustard

Although it is made with kale instead of collard greens, we still like to think of this braised pork panino as a southern flavor standard. You may even consider making it with cornbread for an extra southern touch. The Date Butter is essential to the flavor of this panino, as it adds both sweetness and acidity.

Preheat the press to medium (375°F / 190°C).

Cut kale leaves into ¾-inch (1.8 cm) strips. Melt butter in a saucepan, add kale, and sauté for about 1 minute. Add water, cover pan, and steam for about 2 to 3 minutes, or until cooked. Season to taste with salt and pepper and set aside.

To build each panino, arrange the ingredients in the following order: ciabatta spread with one-quarter Date Butter, kale, Braised Pork, Jack cheese, ciabatta spread with one-quarter Date Butter.

Spread butter on outside of panini (top and bottom) and grill for about 5 to 8 minutes, or until cheese is melted and bread is nicely grilled.

Braised Short Rib, Onion Jam & Stilton Panini

4 slices ciabatta bread, or 2 ciabatta buns, halved

2 Tbsp (30 g) mayonnaise

1 Tbsp (15 g) barbecue sauce

4 Tbsp (60 g) Caramelized Onion Jam (see page 125)

1 recipe Braised Short Ribs (see page 118)

Salt and pepper, to taste

1 oz (30 g) Stilton cheese, crumbled

4 Tbsp (60 g) Pickled Carrots (see page 116) (optional)

Butter, for spreading

ALTERNATIVES

Bread: sourdough or farmer

Cheese: roquefort or Gorgonzola

Meat: pulled pork

Garnish: pickled onions

This panino delivers the classic flavor of pulled meat cooked on a barbecue with no barbecuing involved. The barbecue sauce in the mayonnaise and the Caramelized Onion Jam bring a nice smoky flavor to it. For an extra touch of smoke, you could add a slice or two of grilled bacon. The Pickled Carrots are optional but well worth the time, as they offer a nice touch of acid to contrast with the richness of the beef, along with a crunchy texture.

Preheat the press to medium (375°F/190°C).

In a small bowl, mix mayonnaise and barbecue sauce together.

To build each panino, arrange ingredients in the following order: ciabatta spread with Caramelized Onion Jam, Braised Short Ribs seasoned to taste with salt and pepper, Stilton, Pickled Carrots (if using), ciabatta spread with barbecue-sauce mayonnaise.

Spread butter on outside of panini (top and bottom) and grill for about 5 to 8 minutes, or until cheese is melted and bread is nicely grilled.

Braised Lamb, Olive-Lemon-Bean Mash & Feta Panini

YIELDS 2 PANINI

4 slices ciabatta bread, or 2 ciabatta buns, halved

8 Tbsp (120 g) Olive-Lemon-Bean Mash (see page 123)

4 oz (120 g) Braised Lamb (see page 118)

Salt and pepper, to taste

3 oz (90 g) feta cheese, sliced or crumbled

Butter, for spreading

ALTERNATIVES

Bread: country or farmer

Cheese: hard or soft goat cheese

Meat: roast beef or pork

This panino unites classic flavors of the Mediterranean. If you want to use store-bought hummus, add some chopped olives and lemon zest to taste.

Preheat the press to medium (375°F / 190°C).

To build each panino, arrange ingredients in the following order: ciabatta spread with one-quarter Olive-Lemon-Bean Mash, Braised Lamb seasoned to taste with salt and pepper, feta cheese, ciabatta spread with one-quarter Olive-Lemon-Bean Mash.

Spread butter on outside of panini (top and bottom) and grill for about 5 to 8 minutes, or until cheese is melted and bread is nicely grilled.

Grilled Chicken, Pesto, Red Pepper & Goat Cheese Panini

4 slices ciabatta bread, or 2 ciabatta buns, halved

1 large red pepper, halved and seeded

1 tsp (5 mL) olive oil

4 Tbsp (60 g) Pesto Sauce (see page 122, or store-bought)

4 oz (120 g) roasted chicken

Salt and pepper, to taste

2 oz (60 g) soft goat cheese

Butter, for spreading

ALTERNATIVES

Bread: focaccia or Turkish

Cheese: bocconcini or mozzarella

Meat: roasted turkey

Garnish: grilled onions or zucchini

The classic flavors of chicken and pesto are highlighted in this panino with grilled red pepper and creamy goat cheese. However, if you do not like red pepper, other grilled vegetables will work.

Preheat the press to medium (375°F/190°C).

Brush both sides of red pepper halves with olive oil and cook in the panini press for about 10 to 12 minutes. Remove peppers and set aside.

To build each panino, arrange ingredients in the following order: ciabatta spread with one-quarter Pesto Sauce, chicken seasoned to taste with salt and pepper, red pepper, goat cheese, ciabatta spread with one-quarter Pesto Sauce.

Spread butter on outside of panini (top and bottom) and grill for about 5 to 8 minutes, or until cheese is melted and bread is nicely grilled.

Duck Confit, Yam, Frisée & Roquefort Panini

4 slices ciabatta bread, or 2 ciabatta buns, halved

½ cup (225 g) roasted yam

¼ tsp (1.25 mL) five-spice powder, or to taste

3 oz (90 g) Duck Confit (see page 117)

Salt and pepper, to taste

4 Tbsp (60 g) Pickled Onions (see page 116) (optional)

½ cup (30 g) frisée greens

1 oz (30 g) roquefort cheese, sliced or crumbled

Butter, for spreading

ALTERNATIVES

Bread: country or sourdough

Cheese: Saint Agur or Stilton

Meat: Chinese-style barbecued duck

Greens: dandelion or spinach

The rich Duck Confit, smooth and sweet yam purée, crunchy-acidic Pickled Onions, and creamy-salty roquefort unite in a panino with bold flavors. You could replace the Duck Confit with Chinese-style barbecued duck and omit the yam or replace it with store-bought applesauce for a faster alternative. The Pickled Onions are optional, but well worth the time for the taste contrast and texture they bring.

Preheat the press to medium (375°F / 190°C).

In a bowl, coarsely mash roasted yam and five-spice powder. Set aside.

To build each panino, arrange ingredients in the following order: ciabatta spread with one-quarter roasted yam, Duck Confit seasoned to taste with salt and pepper, Pickled Onions (if using), frisée greens, roquefort cheese, ciabatta spread with one-quarter roasted yam.

Spread butter on outside of panini (top and bottom) and grill for about 5 to 8 minutes, or until cheese is melted and bread is nicely grilled.

Tomato-Bacon-Mushroom & Cheddar "Burger" Panini

4 rounds of raw dough (see page 126), or 4 slices ciabatta bread, or 2 ciabatta buns, halved

6 whole mushrooms, trimmed so stem is level with bottom of cap

1 Tbsp (15 mL) olive oil

1 recipe Roasted Tomatoes (see page 115)

Salt and pepper, to taste

5 oz (150 g) sausage meat

1 oz (30 g) cooked bacon, crumbled

1½ oz (45 g) cheddar cheese, sliced

2 Tbsp (30 mL) olive oil, for brushing (or butter for spreading on bread)

ALTERNATIVES

Bread: country or farmer

Cheese: Emmentaler or Swiss

Meat: ground beef

These are classic burger flavors that work equally well in a panino, especially with the raw-dough option. Roasted Tomatoes add tartness.

Preheat the press to medium (375°F/190°C)

Brush mushroom caps with olive oil and cook in the panini press for approximately 6 to 8 minutes. Remove mushrooms from grill, then slice ¼ inch (6 mm) thick. In a bowl, combine sliced mushrooms with warm Roasted Tomatoes and season with salt and pepper to taste.

Cook sausage meat in a frying pan on high heat for about 3 minutes or until meat is crumbled and cooked throughout.

To build each panino, arrange ingredients in the following order: raw dough or bread, sausage, mushroom-tomato mixture, bacon, cheddar cheese, raw dough or bread. Brush oil on top of raw dough and flip oiled side on the grill, then brush oil on the other side. If using ciabatta, spread butter on outside of panini—top and bottom. Grill for about 5 to 8 minutes, or until cheese is melted and bread is nicely grilled.

CHAPTER 4

Charcuterie & Cured Meats

Ham & Cheese Croque Monsieur Panini

4 slices French bread, or 2 buns, halved

4 Tbsp (80 g) Sauce Béchamel (see page 121), or store-bought alfredo sauce

1 Tbsp (18 g) Dijon mustard

2 Tbsp (12 g) grated Gruyère cheese

Pinch of freshly grated nutmeg, or to taste

2 oz (60 g) Black Forest ham, sliced

2 oz (60 g) Gruyère cheese, sliced

4 tsp (20 mL) finely chopped fresh chives (optional)

Butter, for spreading

ALTERNATIVES

Bread: ciabatta or country

Cheese: Sbrinz or Swiss

Meat: deli roast beef or turkey

Garnish: green onions or parsley

Although a Mornay sauce (béchamel sauce plus cheese) browned under the broiler is the typical way of making this sandwich, we suggest using store-bought alfredo sauce for a quick alternative. Grilling the sandwich as a panino provides a great texture and caramelized flavor.

Preheat the press to medium (375°F/190°C).

For the cheese sauce, combine sauce, mustard, grated cheese, and nutmeg in a small bowl and mix until combined.

To build each panino, arrange ingredients in the following order: bread spread with one-quarter cheese sauce, ham, sliced Gruyère, bread spread with one-quarter cheese sauce, and chives (if using).

Spread butter on outside of panini (top and bottom) and grill for about 5 to 8 minutes, or until cheese is melted and bread is nicely grilled.

Prosciutto, Fig & Provolone Panini

4 slices ciabatta bread, or 2 ciabatta buns, halved

1 medium pear, cut into ½-inch (1.25 cm) slices

1 Tbsp (15 mL) olive oil

4 Tbsp (60 g) Fig Butter (see page 123)

2 oz (60 g) provolone cheese, sliced

2 oz (60 g) prosciutto, sliced

Butter, for spreading

ALTERNATIVES

Bread: country or farmer

Cheese: Asiago or havarti

Meat: coppa or serrano ham

Garnish: store-bought fig or plum jam

The flavor combination of prosciutto, fig, and pear is a time-honored classic. If you do not have time to make the Fig Butter, store-bought fig or plum jam can work, but you will need to add a little balsamic vinegar to balance the sweetness.

Preheat the press to high (440°F/225°C).

Brush pear slices lightly with olive oil and cook in the press for about 3 to 4 minutes, or until pear flesh is soft but slices still hold their shape. Cut into small strips and set aside.

Reduce heat of the press to medium (375°F/190°C).

To build each panino, arrange ingredients in the following order: ciabatta spread with Fig Butter, one-quarter provolone cheese, prosciutto, pear, one-quarter provolone cheese, ciabatta.

Spread butter on outside of panini (top and bottom) and grill for about 5 to 8 minutes, or until cheese is melted and bread is nicely grilled.

Pepperoni, Tomato, Pesto & Bocconcini Panini

YIELDS 2 PANINI

4 rounds of raw dough (see page 126), or 4 slices ciabatta bread, or 2 ciabatta buns, halved

2 Tbsp (30 g) Pesto Sauce (see page 122, or store-bought)

2 oz (60 g) pizza pepperoni

1 recipe Roasted Tomatoes (see page 115)

3 oz (90 g) bocconcini cheese, drained and sliced

2 Tbsp (30 mL) olive oil, for brushing (or butter for spreading on bread)

ALTERNATIVES

Bread: focaccia or Turkish

Cheese: fresh mozzarella

Meat: calabrese or capocollo sausage

Garnish: sun-dried tomatoes

This is a classic flavor combination that works very well with baked bread. Even better, though, is raw bread dough, which turns this classic panino into another classic—calzone, but grilled.

Preheat the press to medium (375°F/190°C).

To build each panino, arrange ingredients in the following order: raw dough or bread spread with Pesto Sauce, pepperoni, Roasted Tomatoes, bocconcini cheese, raw dough or bread.

Brush oil on top of the raw dough and flip oiled side on the grill, then brush oil on the other side. If using ciabatta, spread butter on outside of panini—top and bottom.

Grill panini for about 5 to 8 minutes, or until cheese is melted and bread is cooked and nicely grilled.

Capocollo, Grilled Radicchio & Gruyère Panini

4 slices ciabatta bread, or 2 ciabatta buns, halved

½ cup (80 g) frozen hash browns

½ tsp (2.5 mL) finely chopped fresh rosemary

½ small radicchio

2 tsp (10 mL) olive oil

2 oz (60 g) Gruyère cheese, sliced

2 oz (60 g) capocollo

2 Tbsp (30 mL) horseradish spread

Butter, for spreading

ALTERNATIVES

Bread: country or potato

Cheese: Emmentaler or Swiss

Meat: spicy salami

Garnish: grilled zucchini

Grilled radicchio adds great flavor and texture to this panino. If you cannot find it, grilled zucchini is another option, but use Salsa Verde (see page 122) instead of horseradish.

Preheat the press to medium (375°F/190°C).

Mix hash browns with rosemary and cook following package instructions. Cut radicchio into ½-inch (1.25 cm) slices, brush both sides with olive oil, and cook in the press for 10 to 15 minutes. (If using zucchini, cook the same way, but only for 2 to 4 minutes.)

To build each panino, arrange ingredients in the following order: ciabatta, one-quarter Gruyère, rosemary hash browns, radicchio, capocollo, one-quarter Gruyère, ciabatta spread with horseradish.

Spread butter on outside of panini (top and bottom) and grill for about 5 to 8 minutes, or until cheese is melted and bread is nicely grilled.

Mortadella, Olive-Lemon-Bean Mash & Jarlsberg Panini

YIELDS 2 PANINI

4 slices ciabatta bread, or 2 ciabatta buns, halved

4 Tbsp (60 g) Olive-Lemon-Bean Mash (see page 123)

2 oz (60 g) mortadella

4 Tbsp (60 g) Pickled Onions (see page 116) (optional)

2 oz (60 g) Jarlsberg cheese, sliced

Butter, for spreading

ALTERNATIVES

Bread: country or farmer

Cheese: Edam or Gouda

Meat: bologna or ham

Garnish: baba ghanouj or hummus

If you like hummus, you will love this panino. If you want to use store-bought hummus, add some chopped olive and lemon zest to taste. The Pickled Onions are an option, but well worth the time as they bring an amazing taste and texture!

Preheat the press to medium (375°F / 190°C).

To build each panino, arrange ingredients in the following order: ciabatta spread with one-quarter Olive-Lemon-Bean Mash, mortadella, Pickled Onions (if using), Jarlsberg, ciabatta spread with one-quarter Olive-Lemon-Bean Mash.

Spread butter on outside of bread (top and bottom) and grill for about 5 to 8 minutes, or until cheese is melted and bread is nicely grilled.

Corned Beef, Savoy Cabbage & Smoked Gouda Panini

4 slices ciabatta bread, or 2 ciabatta buns, halved

1 large apple, cut into ½-inch (1.25 cm) slices

1 Tbsp (15 mL) olive oil

2 Tbsp (30 g) butter

2 cups (100 g) Savoy cabbage, julienned

Salt and pepper, to taste

2 Tbsp (30 g) Caramelized Onion Jam (see page 125) (optional)

2 oz (60 g) smoked Gouda cheese, sliced

2 oz (60 g) corned beef

2 Tbsp (30 mL) horseradish spread

Butter, for spreading

ALTERNATIVES

Bread: rye or sourdough

Cheese: regular Gouda or Gruyère

Meat: pastrami or roast beef

Garnish: sauerkraut

This is our take on the classic Reuben sandwich. If you omit the garnish and use sauerkraut instead of cooked cabbage, this panino is exactly what a Reuben sandwich is about.

Preheat the press to medium (375°F / 190°C).

Brush both sides of apple slices lightly with olive oil and cook in the press for about 2 minutes, or until apple flesh is soft but still holding its shape. Cut apple into strips and set aside.

Place 2 Tbsp (30 g) butter in a microwaveable bowl and heat on high for 1 minute or until very hot. Add cabbage and toss well. If cabbage is too crunchy, microwave it briefly to achieve desired doneness. Season to taste with salt and pepper.

To build each panino, arrange ingredients in the following order: ciabatta spread with Caramelized Onion Jam (if using), one-quarter Gouda, grilled apples, corned beef, cooked cabbage, one-quarter Gouda, ciabatta.

Spread butter on outside of panini (top and bottom) and grill for 5 to 8 minutes, or until cheese is melted and bread is nicely grilled.

Pastrami, Braised Red Cabbage & Gorgonzola Panini

YIELDS 2 PANINI

4 slices ciabatta bread, or 2 ciabatta buns, halved

2 oz (60 g) pastrami

⅔ cup (140 g) Braised Red Cabbage (see page 116)

2 oz (60 g) Gorgonzola cheese, sliced

Butter, for spreading

ALTERNATIVES

Bread: rye or sourdough

Cheese: Saint Agur or Stilton

Meat: corned or roast beef

Garnish: grilled or sautéed red cabbage

Although you could use sautéed or grilled red cabbage for this panino, the flavors added—or more precisely, developed—during braising are really what makes this panino comfort food at its best. The smoked note of the meat with the sweet and tart cabbage and salty blue-veined cheese is a match made in heaven.

Preheat the press to medium (375°F/190°C).

To build each panino, arrange ingredients in the following order: ciabatta, pastrami, Braised Red Cabbage, Gorgonzola, ciabatta.

Spread butter on outside of panini (top and bottom) and grill for about 5 to 8 minutes, or until cheese is melted and bread is nicely grilled.

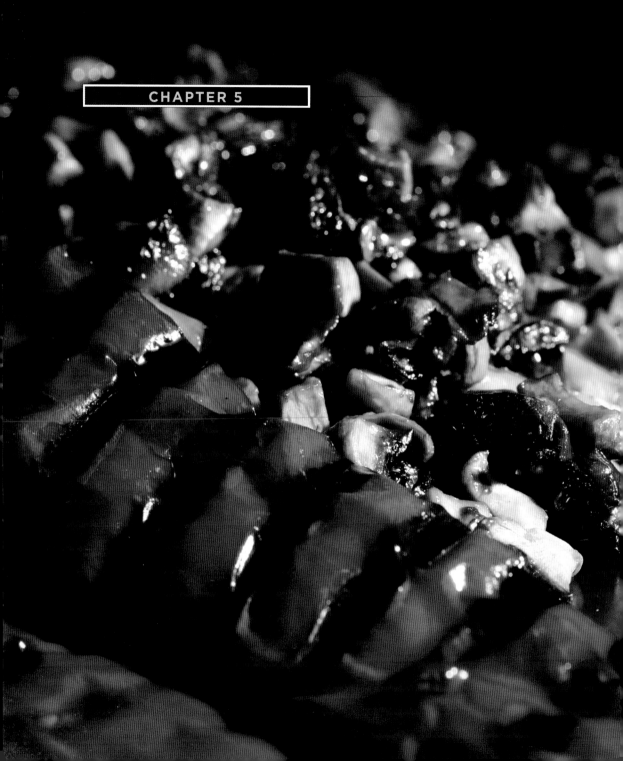

CHAPTER 5

Eggs & Vegetables

Hard-Boiled Egg, Grilled Belgian Endive & Monterey Jack Panini

4 slices ciabatta bread, or 2 ciabatta buns, halved

1 whole Belgian endive

2 tsp (10 mL) olive oil

6 slices bacon, cooked

2 hard-boiled eggs, sliced

1 oz (30 g) Monterey Jack cheese, sliced

4 Tbsp (60 g) Sauce Andalouse (see page 120)

Salt and pepper, to taste

Butter, for spreading

ALTERNATIVES

Bread: *country or farmer*

Cheese: *cheddar or Jarlsberg*

Meat: *back bacon or pancetta*

Sauce: *ketchup*

This is our version of the classic flavor combination of bacon and eggs: breakfast made into a panino. You could make this panino without the endive, but it is well worth the minimal time it requires to prepare as it adds a creamy texture and provides a perfect balance to the richness of the egg and bacon flavors.

Preheat the press to medium (375°F / 190°C).

Cut Belgian endive in half lengthwise and brush both sides with olive oil. Cook in the press for about 15 minutes, or until endive is soft and a knife can pierce it easily.

To build each panino, arrange ingredients in the following order: ciabatta, bacon, egg, Belgian endive, Jack cheese, Sauce Andalouse, ciabatta.

Spread butter on outside of panini (top and bottom) and grill for about 5 to 8 minutes, or until cheese is melted and bread is nicely grilled.

French Ratatouille Frittata & Aged Cheddar Panini

4 slices ciabatta bread, or 2 ciabatta buns, halved

3 large eggs

1 Tbsp (15 mL) olive oil

2 oz (60 g) sausage meat, cooked

½ cup (120 g) Ratatouille (see page 115)

1½ oz (45 g) aged cheddar cheese, sliced

Salt and pepper, to taste

Butter, for spreading

ALTERNATIVES

Bread: *country or farmer*

Cheese: *Asiago or Cantal*

Meat: *cooked ground beef*

Garnish: *Caramelized Onion Jam (see page 125) or Roasted Tomatoes (see page 115)*

Although Ratatouille, with its mixed-vegetable texture and tomatoey sweet-acidic balance, is perfect for this panino, leftover cooked vegetables like peas and carrots could work as well.

Preheat the oven to 400°F (200°C) for the frittata.

Prepare the frittata as shown on page 134, and use sausage meat and Ratatouille as the garnish mixture.

Preheat the press to medium (375°F/190°C).

To build each panino, arrange ingredients in the following order: ciabatta, frittata, cheddar cheese, ciabatta.

Spread butter on outside of panini (top and bottom) and grill for about 5 to 8 minutes, or until cheese is melted and bread is nicely grilled.

Oven-Fried Egg, Baby Spinach & Duck Confit Panini

YIELDS 2 PANINI

4 slices ciabatta bread, or 2 ciabatta buns, halved

1 Tbsp (15 mL) olive oil

2 large eggs

Salt and pepper, to taste

3 oz (90 g) Duck Confit (see page 117, or store-bought), shredded

½ cup (30 g) baby spinach leaves

2 oz (60 g) brie cheese

Butter, for spreading

ALTERNATIVES

Bread: sourdough or country

Cheese: vacherin or Camembert

Meat: Chinese-style barbecued duck or pork

Garnish: frisée or dandelion greens

Duck Confit, with its rich flavor and texture, is a great addition to this panino. Lacquered Peking-style duck, char siu pork, or even store-bought rotisserie chicken would work well too.

Preheat the oven to 400°F (200°C).

Prepare oven-fried egg: Place oil in an 8- × 4-inch (20 × 10 cm) loaf pan and heat for about 6 to 10 minutes, or until oil is very hot. Crack 1 egg into a small cup and carefully pour it into the pan, being careful not to break the yolk. Repeat for second egg. Cook for approximately 6 to 10 minutes, or until eggs are cooked to your preferred doneness. Remove eggs from the loaf pan, cut or separate the 2 eggs, season to taste with salt and pepper, and keep warm. (Alternatively, eggs can be pan-fried on the stove top.)

Preheat the press to medium (375°F/190°C).

To build each panino, arrange ingredients in the following order: ciabatta, Duck Confit, spinach, brie, egg, ciabatta.

Spread butter on outside of panini (top and bottom) and grill for about 5 to 8 minutes, or until cheese is melted and bread is nicely grilled.

Curried Chickpea, Roasted Eggplant & Chicken Panini

4 rounds of raw dough (see page 126), or 4 slices ciabatta bread, or 2 ciabatta buns, halved

1 small Japanese eggplant

4 tsp + 1 Tbsp (35 mL) olive oil

½ cup (80 g) canned chickpeas, rinsed and drained

1 tsp (5 mL) Madras curry powder, or to taste

4 oz (120 g) roasted or rotisserie chicken, shredded

2 oz (60 g) pecorino cheese, grated

Salt and pepper, to taste

2 Tbsp (30 mL) olive oil, for brushing (or butter for spreading on bread)

ALTERNATIVES

Bread: *Turkish*

Cheese: *paneer or Swiss*

Meat: *deli-style chicken or turkey*

We suggest using raw bread dough, which turns this panino into an incredible combination of fresh-baked bread aroma and stuffed-bread texture.

Preheat the press to medium (375°F / 190°C).

Slice eggplant in half lengthwise and brush both sides with 4 tsp (20 mL) olive oil. Cook eggplant in the press for about 6 minutes, or until the flesh is soft. Remove from grill and let eggplant cool before removing skin and coarsely chopping the flesh. In a large bowl, mash chickpeas with a fork, then add chopped eggplant, 1 Tbsp (15 mL) olive oil, and curry powder, mixing until combined.

To build each panino, arrange ingredients in the following order: raw dough or bread spread with chickpea mixture, chicken, pecorino, raw dough or bread.

Brush oil on top of raw dough and flip oiled side on the grill, then brush oil on the other side. If using ciabatta, spread butter on the outside—top and bottom. Grill for 5 to 8 minutes or until cheese is melted and bread is nicely grilled.

Baked Eggs, Mushroom-Tomato Roast & Ham Panini

YIELDS 2 PANINI

4 slices ciabatta bread, or 2 ciabatta buns, halved

6 medium cremini mushrooms, or 2 small portobello mushrooms, stems trimmed

1 Tbsp (15 mL) olive oil

1 recipe Roasted Tomatoes (see page 115), warm

Salt and pepper, to taste

3 large eggs

1 Tbsp (15 mL) olive oil

2 oz (60 g) smoked ham

2 oz (60 g) Asiago cheese

2 Tbsp (30 g) Salsa Verde (see page 122)

2 Tbsp (30 g) butter

ALTERNATIVES

Bread: country or sourdough

Cheese: bocconcini or mozzarella

Meat: deli-style smoked meat

Sauce: Pesto Sauce (see page 122)

The balance of the meaty roasted mushroom texture, sweet-acidic flavor from the tomatoes, and smoky notes from the ham is great in this panino. Leftover cooked vegetables, such as peas and carrots, could be also used instead of the mushrooms.

Preheat the oven to 400°F (200°C).

Preheat the press to medium (375°F/190°C).

For the roasted mushrooms, brush mushrooms with 1 Tbsp (15 mL) olive oil. Cook mushrooms in the press for 6 to 8 minutes. Remove and slice ¼ inch (6 mm) thick. In a bowl, combine sliced mushrooms with warm Roasted Tomatoes and season to taste with salt and pepper.

Prepare the eggs as shown on page 134 and use mushroom tomato roast as garnish mixture.

To build each panino, arrange ingredients in the following order: ciabatta, Salsa Verde, baked eggs, ham, Asiago, ciabatta.

Spread butter on the outside of the panini (top and bottom) and grill for 5 to 8 minutes, or until cheese is melted and bread is nicely grilled.

Hash Brown–Arugula Frittata & Fontina Panini

4 slices ciabatta bread, or 2 ciabatta buns, halved

3 large eggs

1 Tbsp (15 mL) olive oil

1.5 oz (45 g) soppressata, cut into 1-inch (2.5 cm) squares

½ cup (80 g) frozen hash browns, cooked according to package instructions

4 Tbsp (60 g) Salsa Verde (see page 122)

½ cup (30 g) arugula

1 oz (30 g) Fontina cheese, sliced

Butter, for spreading

ALTERNATIVES

Bread: country or potato

Cheese: Edam or Gouda

Meat: calabrese or other salami

Sauce: Pesto Sauce (see page 122)

Garnish: baby spinach or dandelion greens

The mixture of crispy fried potatoes, peppery arugula, creamy Salsa Verde, and classic soppressata salami turns this panino into a hearty and comforting meal. Note that just about any salami will work, and so would leftover roasted potatoes instead of hash browns.

Preheat the oven to 400°F (200°C) for the frittata.

Prepare the eggs as shown on page 134 and use soppressata and hash browns as the garnish mixture.

Preheat the press to medium (375°F/190°C).

To build each panino, arrange ingredients in the following order: ciabatta spread with one-quarter Salsa Verde, frittata, arugula, Fontina, ciabatta spread with one-quarter Salsa Verde.

Spread butter on the outside of the panini (top and bottom) and grill for 5 to 8 minutes, or until cheese is melted and bread is nicely grilled.

Sweets & Fruits

Nutella, Orange Marmalade & Raspberry Panini

4 slices white bread

2 Tbsp (40 g) Nutella

32 fresh raspberries

2 Tbsp (40 g) orange marmalade, store-bought

Butter, for spreading

ALTERNATIVES

Bread: brioche or challah

Nut butter: almond or peanut

Garnish: blackberries or strawberries

This is our version of the classic PBJ sandwich, and of course you can turn it back into the classic by replacing the Nutella with peanut butter. However, the harmony between the chocolate-nut flavor of the Nutella, orange from the marmalade, and slight acidity of fresh raspberries really adds a new level of complexity in terms of taste and texture.

Preheat the press to medium (375°F/190°C).

To build each panino, arrange ingredients in the following order: bread spread with Nutella, raspberries, bread spread with marmalade.

Spread butter on outside of panini (top and bottom) and grill for about 3 to 4 minutes, or until bread is nicely grilled.

Raisin Bread French Toast & Apricot Butter Panini

4 slices raisin bread

2 large eggs

2 Tbsp (30 mL) milk

1 recipe Apricot Butter (see page 124)

Icing sugar, for dusting (optional)

ALTERNATIVES

Bread: challah or brioche

Fruit: orange marmalade

The French classic *pain perdu* ("lost bread"), much loved by children, is typically served topped with powdered sugar and jam on the side. We wanted to make the classic into a panino, so we came up with the idea of stuffing the bread with a jamlike filling, but without the added sugar. This option still provides all of the flavor of the classic, but with a new texture twist. For an extra touch of flavor, add a pinch of saffron to the Apricot Butter—just amazing!

Preheat the press to medium (375°F/190°C).

In a bowl, or shallow dish, whisk eggs and milk together until combined.

To build each panino, spread Apricot Butter on bottom slice of bread, top with second slice of bread, and soak in egg mixture for about 10 to 15 seconds on each side. Place on a serving plate.

Grill panini for about 3 to 4 minutes, or until egg mixture is cooked and bread is nicely grilled. Dust with icing sugar, if using.

Coconut Mascarpone Cream & Banana Bread Panini

≡ YIELDS 2 PANINI ≡

1 large banana, peeled

2 Tbsp (40 g) Pastry Cream (see page 119), warm

1 Tbsp (8 g) toasted sweetened coconut, finely ground

1 oz (30 g) mascarpone cheese

4 slices Banana Bread (see page 132), ½ inch (1.25 cm) thick

1 tsp (5 g) granulated sugar

Unsalted butter, for spreading

ALTERNATIVES

Cake: *coffee cake or pound cake*

Fruit: *blueberries or pineapple*

The inspiration for this panino is drawn from the classic banana-coconut cream pie. The crispy bread is like a crust to the silky smooth mascarpone cheese–cream filling that is covered with fresh bananas. As an option, serve with whipped cream or extra cream filling topped with toasted coconut.

Preheat the press to medium (375°F/190°C).

Cut banana in half and heat one half in a microwaveable container for about 45 to 60 seconds on high, until soft and hot. In the bowl of a food processor, combine hot banana, warm Pastry Cream, coconut, and mascarpone cheese, and blend until combined and smooth. Just before serving, cut remaining banana half into thin slices and set aside.

To build each panino, arrange ingredients in the following order: Banana Bread spread with one-quarter cream mixture, banana slices, sprinkling of sugar, Banana Bread spread with one-quarter cream mixture.

Spread butter on outside of panini (top and bottom) and grill for about 3 to 4 minutes, or until Banana Bread is nicely grilled.

Almond Raisin Butter, Apple & Croissant Panini

1 large apple, cut into ½-inch (1.25 cm) slices

1 Tbsp (15 mL) olive oil

2 Tbsp (40 g) apricot jam, store-bought

¼ tsp (1.25 mL) finely grated fresh ginger

4 Tbsp (60 g) Almond Raisin Butter
(see page 124)

2 croissants, halved

ALTERNATIVES

Bread: brioche or challah

Cream: custard

Fruit: nectarine or pear

The inspiration for this panino is a French classic: puff-pastry apple tart. When cooked in the panini press, the flaky croissant is very similar in texture to puff-pastry dough, while the Almond Raisin Butter provides a creamy texture that equals the almond cream. All in all, this panino is a quick version of the French classic, with almost identical taste and texture but ready in just a few minutes!

Preheat the press to medium (375°F/190°C).

Lightly brush apple slices with olive oil on both sides. Cook in the press for about 2 minutes, or until apple is soft but still holding its shape. Cut apple into ½-inch (1.25 cm) cubes or strips and set aside. In a small bowl, mix apricot jam and ginger until well combined.

To build each panino, arrange ingredients in the following order: croissant spread with Almond Raisin Butter, apple, croissant spread with ginger-apricot jam.

Grill panini for about 2 minutes, or until croissant is nicely grilled and crispy.

Balsamic Neufchâtel Cream & Strawberry Panini

1 oz (30 g) Neufchâtel cheese

2 Tbsp (40 g) strawberry jam

Few drops of aged balsamic vinegar

4 slices Pound Cake (see page 131),
½ inch (1.25 cm) thick

4 large fresh strawberries, sliced

2 large basil leaves (optional)

Unsalted butter, for spreading

ALTERNATIVES

Cake: *coffee cake or sponge cake*

Cheese: *cream cheese*

Like fish and chips, figs and Port, and melon and prosciutto, strawberries and cream is a time-honored classic flavor combination. In this panino, the Neufchâtel cheese takes the place of the cream. For a little touch of taste luxury, add a few drops of well-aged balsamic vinegar (12 years or older). The vinegar works beautifully to enhance the flavor of the strawberries.

Preheat the press to medium (375°F / 190°C).

In a bowl, whisk together Neufchâtel, jam, and balsamic vinegar until well combined.

To build each panino, arrange ingredients in the following order: cake spread with one-quarter Neufchâtel mixture, strawberries, basil leaf (if using), cake spread with one-quarter Neufchâtel mixture.

Spread butter on outside of panini (top and bottom) and grill for about 2 to 3 minutes, or until cake is nicely grilled.

Kirsch Cream, Cherry & Chocolate Cake Panini

4 Tbsp (80 g) Pastry Cream (see page 119), warm

1.4 oz (40 g) 70% dark chocolate, melted

1 tsp (5 mL) kirsch, or to taste

16 cherries, canned or fresh, halved

4 slices Devil's Food Cake (see page 131), ½ inch (1.25 cm) thick

ALTERNATIVES

Cake: chocolate sponge

Fruit: blackberries or raspberries

This sweet panino unites the flavors of classic Black Forest cake, but this is a warm and crispy version. The only classic element missing is the whipped cream, which we highly recommend serving on the side. For an even better contrast, serve the panino with a high-quality vanilla ice cream made with cream, which will provide the classic taste, but at a different temperature.

Preheat the press to medium (375°F/190°C).

In a small bowl, whisk together warm Pastry Cream and melted chocolate until combined. Add kirsch and continue whisking until the mixture is smooth.

To build each panino, arrange ingredients in the following order: cake spread with one-quarter chocolate cream, cherries, cake spread with one-quarter chocolate cream.

Grill panini for about 2 minutes, or until cake is lightly grilled.

Orange Cream & Caramel Crêpe Panini

YIELDS 2 LARGE OR 4 SMALL

4 Tbsp (80 g) Pastry Cream (see page 119), warm

Zest of ¼ orange

1 Tbsp (20 g) orange marmalade, store-bought

6 large store-bought crêpes, or 12 small (3-inch/7.5 cm) French Crêpes (see page 130), preferably cooked in a square pan

2 Tbsp (30 g) granulated sugar

1 Tbsp (15 g) butter, melted

ALTERNATIVES

Fruit: grapefruit or lemon

Jam: apricot or peach

Crêpes Suzette is a classic French dessert that is made tableside in restaurants and served with a sauce made from caramelized sugar and oranges. This panino provides the same flavor profile, but with a caramel texture. The crêpes are brushed with butter and sugar; then the high heat of the grill quickly caramelizes the sugar—giving the panini a thin and crunchy exterior.

Preheat the press to high (440°F/225°C).

In a bowl, whisk together warm Pastry Cream, orange zest, and marmalade until well combined.

To build each panino, spread a thin layer of orange cream on the bottom crêpe, lay another crêpe on top and spread with another thin layer of cream. Repeat this process until you have 2 stacks (each with 3 large crêpes) or 4 stacks (each with 6 small ones).

Just before serving, brush top and bottom crêpes lightly with melted butter and sprinkle both with sugar. Grill sugared crêpes on high heat for about 2 minutes, or until sugar is caramelized but not burnt.

Almond Cream, Peach, Raspberry & Pound Cake Panini

2 Tbsp (40 g) Pastry Cream (see page 119), warm

1 Tbsp (9 g) ground toasted almonds

4 slices Pound Cake (see page 131), ½ inch (1.25 cm) thick

4 slices canned peaches, halved

12 fresh raspberries, halved

Unsalted butter, for spreading

ALTERNATIVES

Cake: chiffon or sponge

Fruit: apricots, nectarines, or strawberries

The traditional dessert peach Melba, invented by French chef Auguste Escoffier, is the foundation of this panino. The classic is made with raspberry sauce, but we found that fresh raspberries cooked in the panini press provide a similar alternative, and are fresher and much faster to prepare. As with the classic, this panino would be great served with a scoop of vanilla ice cream.

Preheat the press to medium (375°F/190°C).

In a small bowl, whisk together warm Pastry Cream and ground almonds until combined.

To build each panino, arrange ingredients in the following order: cake, peach slices, raspberries, cake spread with almond pastry cream.

Spread butter on outside of panini (top and bottom) and grill for about 2 minutes, or until cake is lightly grilled.

Almond Ricotta Cream, Craisin & Panettone Panini

2 slices panettone

3 Tbsp (45 g) ricotta cheese

1 Tbsp (9 g) finely chopped toasted almonds

1 Tbsp (12 g) finely chopped dried cranberries

Seeds of 1 vanilla bean

1 tsp (8 g) liquid honey

Zest of ½ lemon

Butter, for spreading

2 tsp (10 g) granulated sugar

ALTERNATIVES

Bread: brioche or challah

Fruit: dried blueberries or raisins

Crostata di ricotta, the classic Italian cheese dessert, was our inspiration for this panino, though we added our own touch. You can use other dried fruits or nuts if desired. A pinch of cinnamon or a bit of freshly grated nutmeg would be a suitable alternative to the vanilla bean seeds.

Preheat the press to medium (375°F/190°C).

In a small bowl, combine ricotta, chopped almonds, dried cranberries, vanilla bean seeds, honey, and lemon zest.

To build each panino, spread cheese filling on a slice of panettone and fold in half.

Spread butter on outside of panini (top and bottom) and sprinkle both sides with sugar. Grill for about 2 to 3 minutes, or until sugar is caramelized but not burnt.

Lemon Cream, Sponge Toffee & Scotch Pancake Panini

8 Scotch Pancakes (see page 129)

4 Tbsp (80 g) Pastry Cream (see page 119), warm

1 Tbsp (15 g) butter, softened

Zest of ½ lemon

1 tsp (5 mL) lemon juice

1 oz (28 g) Sponge Toffee (page 133 or store-bought), chopped

ALTERNATIVES

Cake: English-style crumpets

Fruit: grapefruit or orange

This sweet panino is all about texture. The airy Scotch Pancakes, grilled crisp on the outside with a soft center, contrast perfectly with the luscious lemon cream dotted with the syrupy sponge toffee. For extra texture, serve with some crunchy toffee on top.

Preheat the press to medium (375°F / 190°C).

Prepare the lemon cream: In a small bowl, whisk together warm Pastry Cream, butter, lemon zest, and lemon juice.

To build each panino, arrange ingredients in the following order: pancake spread with one-eighth lemon cream, enough Sponge Toffee to just cover, pancake spread with one-eighth lemon cream.

Grill for about 2 minutes, or until pancakes are nicely grilled.

Honey, Pecan, Pear, Blue Cheese Cream & Brioche Panini

4 slices brioche bread, or 2 brioche buns, halved

1 medium pear, cut into ½-inch (1.25 cm) slices

1 Tbsp (15 mL) olive oil, or other fruit or nut oil

½ oz (15 g) cream cheese

½ oz (15 g) blue-veined cheese

2 Tbsp (16 g) chopped toasted pecans

2 tsp (15 g) liquid honey

Unsalted butter, for spreading

2 tsp (10 g) granulated sugar

ALTERNATIVES

Bread: challah or milk bread

Fruit: apple or fig

Blue cheese has long been considered a classic pairing with tree fruits such as pears, apples, or figs; a touch of honey; and roasted—or better yet caramelized—nuts such as almonds, hazelnuts, pecans, or walnuts. For this panino, any combination of these ingredients would work equally well.

Preheat the press to high (440°F/225°C).

Brush pear slices lightly with oil and cook in the press for about 3 to 4 minutes, until pear flesh is soft but slices still hold their shape.

Reduce heat of the press to medium (375°F/190°C).

In a small bowl, mix blue cheese and cream cheese until smooth. Add pecans and honey and continue mixing until combined.

To build each panino, arrange ingredients in the following order: brioche spread with blue cheese cream, pear, brioche.

Spread butter on outside of panini (top and bottom) and sprinkle both sides with sugar. Grill for about 2 to 3 minutes, or until sugar is caramelized but not burnt.

Peanut Butter, Mango & Roasted Macadamia Nut Panini

4 slices Banana Bread (see page 132), ½ inch (1.25 cm) thick

2 Tbsp (60 g) peanut butter

4 whole macadamia nuts, toasted and coarsely chopped

½ medium mango, thinly sliced

1 Tbsp (20 g) blackberry jam

Unsalted butter, for spreading

ALTERNATIVES

Bread: country or white

Nut butter: almond or macadamia nut

Fruit: nectarine or peach

This panino is an upscale variation of the traditional peanut butter and jelly sandwich. The soft fresh mango and crunchy roasted macadamia nuts add a new level of texture contrast to the classic, while the blackberry jam provides additional flavor depth. And it is all made even more complex by the use of Banana Bread instead of the standard white bread.

Preheat the press to medium (375°F/190°C).

To build each panino, arrange ingredients in the following order: Banana Bread spread with peanut butter, macadamia nuts, mango, Banana Bread spread with blackberry jam.

Spread butter on outside of panini (top and bottom) and grill for about 3 to 4 minutes, or until Banana Bread is nicely grilled.

CHAPTER 7

Basic Recipes

Vegetables

RATATOUILLE

Yields about 3½ cups (750 g)

Cut vegetables into ½-inch (1.25 cm) cubes. Cook each vegetable separately in a saucepan on high heat, using 1 Tbsp (15 mL) olive oil for each vegetable, to desired doneness. Set cooked vegetables aside in a large bowl until all vegetables are done.

Season cooked vegetables with salt and pepper, add garlic, Roasted Tomatoes (or ketchup), parsley, and thyme, and toss to coat. Pour all ingredients back into saucepan and cook on low heat for a few minutes to blend the flavors and cook the garlic.

Use warm or keep refrigerated in a container with a tight-fitting lid for up to 3 days.

1 medium-sized red pepper
6 button mushrooms
1 medium-sized zucchini
1 small Japanese eggplant
1 medium-sized onion
5 Tbsp (75 mL) olive oil, divided
Salt and pepper, to taste
3 cloves garlic, finely chopped
3 Tbsp (45 g) Roasted Tomatoes (below), or ketchup
1 Tbsp (15 mL) chopped parsley
2 to 3 sprigs fresh thyme, leaves only

ROASTED TOMATOES

Yields about 1 cup (150 g)

Set the oven to broil.

In a bowl, combine all ingredients and toss lightly. Arrange tomatoes cut side down on a baking sheet and broil for 2 to 3 minutes, or until tomatoes are soft but still hold their shape.

16 grape tomatoes, halved
1 Tbsp (15 mL) olive oil
1 clove garlic, finely chopped
2 sprigs fresh thyme, chopped
Salt and pepper, to taste

BRAISED RED CABBAGE

Yields about 2 cups (400 g)

2 Tbsp (30 g) finely chopped onion
3 Tbsp (45 g) butter
2 Tbsp (24 g) dried cranberries
¼ whole red cabbage, chopped
1 cup (250 mL) red wine
1 Tbsp (15 g) barbecue sauce
1 cup (250 mL) water
½ tsp (2.5 mL) balsamic vinegar
Salt and pepper, to taste

In a sauté pan, cook onion and butter on high heat for about 1 minute. Add cranberries and cabbage and cook for another 5 minutes. Add red wine, barbecue sauce, and water. Reduce heat to medium-low and cover with a lid. Cook for about 50 to 55 minutes, or until all liquid has evaporated and cabbage is cooked. Add vinegar and season to taste with salt and pepper.

As an option, you can cook the cabbage much faster using a pressure cooker. Place all ingredients (omitting the water) in the pressure cooker and cook for 3 minutes from the time the vessel reaches pressure. After 3 minutes, release pressure and open the lid to stop cooking.

PICKLED VEGETABLES

Yields 1 cup (150 g)

½ cup (125 mL) water
½ cup (125 mL) rice vinegar
1 Tbsp (15 mL) kosher salt
1 clove garlic
1 tsp (5 mL) mustard seeds
1 tsp (5 mL) black peppercorns
1 tsp (5 mL) chopped fresh ginger
½ tsp (2.5 mL) chili flakes
½ lemon, zest and juice
1 cup thinly sliced vegetables (e.g., onion, fennel bulb, carrot)

In a saucepan with a tight-fitting lid, combine all ingredients except for the vegetables and bring to a boil. Remove from heat, cover, and let stand for at least 1 hour (overnight is best).

Strain mixture, pour over vegetables, and store in refrigerator at least overnight (24 hours is best) in a sealed Ziploc bag or a tightly sealed jar.

Pickled Vegetables can be stored in the refrigerator for up to 2 weeks.

Meats

MEAT CONFIT
Yields about 2 cups (500 g)

"Confit" refers to meat that is cured, then cooked slowly and preserved in its own fat. This method is intended to preserve meat for longer periods of time. Curing the meat in salt first for 12 hours draws the moisture away from it and thus reduces the water content, making it less likely that microorganisms will grow and spoil the meat after cooking. Storing the cooked meat in its own fat provides an additional barrier against air, again preventing spoilage and extending shelf life.

CURING: Rinse meat under cold running water and pat dry with paper towel. Rub salt on all sides of meat, then place on top of sliced garlic in a large baking dish. Cover dish with a lid or plastic wrap and place in refrigerator to cure overnight (at least 12 hours).

COOKING: Rinse cured meat under cold running water and pat dry with paper towel. Place meat in cooking vessel (slow cooker, cast iron pot, or roasting pan), then add remaining ingredients. Cover and cook until meat is very tender and pulls away to expose the bones, about 6 to 8 hours in a slow cooker on low, or 3 to 4 hours in the oven at 170°F to 250°F (76°C to 120°C). Monitor the heat, and reduce it if the fat creates more than one or two bubbles a minute.

When meat is done, remove from the fat and serve immediately, or place dish on a wire rack to cool. Strain off fat into a bowl and discard aromatics. Pick the meat from the bones and

CURING

2 lb (1 kg) bone-in meat (e.g., 4 duck or chicken legs with thighs attached)
2 Tbsp (40 g) coarse salt
5 cloves garlic, sliced

COOKING

8 sprigs fresh thyme
2 bay leaves
1 Tbsp (15 mL) black peppercorns
1 tsp (5 mL) juniper berries
5 cloves garlic
4 cups (1 L) olive oil

place in a clean stoneware container or glass jar. Pour enough strained fat over meat to cover by at least ¼ inch (6 mm), then store covered in the refrigerator for up to 1 month.

To use the confit, remove it from the refrigerator and let it sit at room temperature until the fat has become liquid, about 1 hour.

NOTE: The extra fat can be used again for confit, or as regular cooking fat.

BRAISED MEAT
Yields about 1 cup (250 g)

1 lb (500 g) meat (e.g., short ribs, lamb, pork)

Bouquet garni (1 bay leaf, 1 sprig fresh thyme, 1 sprig parsley)

1 Tbsp (15 mL) olive oil

1 carrot, coarsely chopped

½ medium-sized onion, coarsely chopped

1 clove garlic

¼ cup (60 mL) red wine

¼ tsp (1.25 mL) black peppercorns, or to taste

¼ tsp (1.25 mL) coarse salt, or to taste

Water, to cover

Preheat the oven to 300°F (150°C).

Preheat the press to high (440°F / 225°C).

Cook meat in the press for about 5 minutes, or until caramelized.

Transfer cooked meat to a roasting pan and add remaining ingredients. Cover the pan with aluminum foil. Roast meat in the oven for 2½ to 3 hours, or until fork-tender.

NOTE: For additional flavor, use beef, chicken, or vegetable stock instead of water.

Creams & Sauces

PASTRY CREAM
Yields about 1¼ cups (375 g)

Scald milk with about half the sugar in a heavy saucepan. In a bowl, vigorously whisk remaining sugar with custard powder and egg until mixture is smooth and creamy. Pour hot milk into egg mixture a little at a time, whisking constantly. Strain combined mixture back into the saucepan. Cook mixture on high heat until it forms bubbles and thickens, stirring constantly with a wire whisk to prevent scorching.

Remove from heat, transfer to a clean container, and use warm as per recipe. Or cover immediately with plastic wrap, pressed against the cream. Using the sharp point of a knife, puncture about 6 holes in the plastic to allow steam to escape. Cool and refrigerate for up to 3 or 4 days. To rewarm, heat gently in the microwave on low heat, stirring frequently.

1 cup (250 mL) 2% milk
¼ cup + 2 tsp (60 g) granulated sugar
3 Tbsp + 2 tsp (25 g) custard powder, or cornstarch
1 large egg

CITRUS AIOLI
Yields about ¼ cup (60 g)

Combine all ingredients in a food processor and mix until smooth.

Store refrigerated in a container with a tight-fitting lid for up to 1 week.

¼ cup (60 g) mayonnaise
1 tsp (5 mL) citrus zest
2 Tbsp (30 g) roasted garlic

FLAVORED MAYONNAISE

Yields about ¼ cup (60 g)

¼ cup (60 g) mayonnaise

Flavoring sauce (2 Tbsp/30 g) or spice powder (1 to 2 tsp/5 to 10 mL)

Flavoring sauces include any homemade or store-bought sauces such as barbecue, Thai sweet chili, hoisin, and pesto. Flavoring powders include spices (single or mixed) such as ancho chili, curry, and garam masala. Vary the amount depending on your taste preferences.

Whisk together mayonnaise and flavoring, or blend in a food processor, until smooth.

Store refrigerated in a container with a tight-fitting lid for up to 1 week.

SAUCE ANDALOUSE

Yields about ⅓ cup (80 g)

1 tsp (5 mL) olive oil
2 Tbsp (20 g) finely chopped onions
2 Tbsp (24 g) finely chopped red pepper
¼ cup (60 g) mayonnaise
1 Tbsp (15 g) tomato paste
Salt, to taste
Ancho chili powder, to taste

Heat olive oil in a saucepan on medium-high heat. Add onion and red pepper and cook until soft. Let cool.

In a bowl, mix mayonnaise and tomato paste until well combined, add cooked vegetables, and continue mixing until incorporated. Season to taste with salt and ancho chili.

Store refrigerated in a container with a tight-fitting lid for up to 1 week.

SAUCE BÉCHAMEL

Yields about 1 cup (250 g)

Heat milk in a saucepan until almost boiling. Remove from heat. Add onion and bay leaf, cover with a tight-fitting lid, and let infuse for at least 30 minutes. In another saucepan, melt butter on low heat, add flour, and cook while whisking for about 1 to 2 minutes, or until mixture is homogenous. Remove from heat and discard onion and bay leaf from milk, then gradually add the infused milk to the flour-butter mixture while whisking continuously. Continue cooking on medium-high heat until all ingredients are incorporated and the sauce is thick. Season to taste with salt and pepper.

Remove from heat and transfer to a clean container. Use warm or cover container immediately with plastic wrap, pressed right against the cream. Using the sharp point of a knife, puncture about 6 holes in the plastic to allow steam to escape. Cool and refrigerate for up to 3 or 4 days.

1 cup (250 mL) milk
One layer onion
1 bay leaf
2 Tbsp (30 g) butter
2 Tbsp (20 g) all-purpose flour
Salt and pepper, to taste

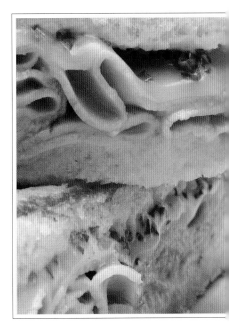

PESTO SAUCE

Yields about 1 cup (250 g)

2 cups (120 g) fresh basil leaves
(packed), chopped

⅓ cup (50 g) chopped pine nuts,
or walnuts

3 cloves garlic, chopped

Pinch of ascorbic acid (optional)

½ cup (125 mL) extra virgin olive oil

½ cup (40 g) freshly grated
Parmesan cheese

Salt and pepper, to taste

Combine basil, nuts, garlic, and ascorbic acid (if using) in a food processor and pulse a few times until all ingredients are combined. Add the olive oil in a constant stream while the machine is running. Stop the machine, add Parmesan, and pulse again until blended. Season to taste with salt and pepper.

Store refrigerated in a container with a tight-fitting lid for up to 1 week.

SALSA VERDE

Yields about ¾ cup (190 g)

2 cups (55 g) chopped parsley

1 Tbsp (15 g) chopped shallots

4 cloves garlic, chopped

1 Tbsp (20 g) capers, chopped

¼ cup (60 mL) olive oil

1 Tbsp (15 mL) white wine vinegar

½ tsp (2.5 mL) kosher salt

½ tsp (2.5 mL) freshly ground
black pepper

Pinch of ascorbic acid (optional)

Place the ingredients in a food processor and pulse several times until all ingredients are well combined.

Keep refrigerated in a container with a tight-fitting lid for up to 1 week.

Butters & Spreads

OLIVE-LEMON-BEAN MASH

Yields about 1½ cups (500 g)

In a food processor, blend chickpeas, lemon zest, lemon juice, olive oil, and garlic until ingredients form a smooth paste. Add kalamata olives and pulse until just mixed in. Season to taste with salt and pepper.

Store refrigerated in a container with a tight-fitting lid for up to 1 week.

NOTE: This recipe makes more than needed for 2 panini. However, the extra mixture can be used as a spread for crackers or bread, or as a dip for chips.

19 oz (540 mL) can chickpeas, rinsed and drained
Zest of 1 lemon
Juice of ½ lemon
½ cup (125 mL) olive oil
2 cloves garlic
½ cup (100 g) kalamata olives, pits removed, chopped
Salt and pepper, to taste

FIG OR DATE BUTTER

Yields about ½ cup (130 g)

In a microwaveable container, combine figs or dates with sherry and cook on high heat for about 2 minutes, or until fruit has absorbed nearly all of the liquid. Transfer hot mixture to a food processor, add remaining ingredients, and blend until ingredients are combined and mixture is smooth.

Store refrigerated in a container with a tight-fitting lid for up to 1 week.

8 whole black mission figs, quartered, or 10 whole dates, quartered
3 Tbsp (45 mL) sherry
½ tsp (2.5 mL) 12-year-old balsamic vinegar
Salt and pepper, to taste
Pinch of ground star anise
4 tsp (30 g) chopped sun-dried tomato
2 Tbsp (30 g) butter

APRICOT BUTTER

Yields about ½ cup (100 g)

6 whole dried apricots, cut into quarters
2 Tbsp (30 mL) water
Pinch of saffron, or to taste (optional)
2 Tbsp (30 g) unsalted butter

In a microwaveable container, combine apricots, water, and saffron (if using) and cook on high heat for about 2 minutes, or until fruit has absorbed nearly all of the water. Transfer mixture to a food processor, add butter, and blend until ingredients are combined and mixture is smooth.

Store refrigerated in a container with a tight-fitting lid for up to 1 week.

ALMOND RAISIN BUTTER

Yields about ⅔ cup (170 g)

⅓ cup (50 g) raisins
2 Tbsp (30 mL) water
½ cup (65 g) chopped toasted almonds
2 Tbsp (30 g) unsalted butter

In a microwaveable container, combine raisins with water and cook on high heat for about 2 minutes, or until raisins have absorbed nearly all of the water. Transfer mixture to a food processor, add almonds and butter, and blend until ingredients are combined and mixture is smooth.

Store refrigerated in a container with a tight-fitting lid until needed, or for up to 1 week.

CARAMELIZED ONION JAM

Yields about 1 cup (250 g)

Combine onions, star anise, water, brown sugar, vegetable oil, and hoisin sauce in a saucepan. Cover and cook mixture on medium-high heat, stirring occasionally, for about 30 minutes, or until the water has evaporated. Remove from heat and discard star anise, then continue cooking on high heat until onion mixture starts to brown, or caramelize. Remove from heat, add balsamic vinegar, and season to taste with salt and pepper.

Use warm, or store refrigerated in a container with a tight-fitting lid for up to 1 week.

3 medium-sized onions, finely sliced
2 whole star anise
1 cup (250 mL) water
2 Tbsp (30 g) brown sugar, packed
3 Tbsp (45 mL) vegetable oil
2 Tbsp (30 mL) hoisin sauce
½ tsp (2.5 mL) 12-year-old balsamic vinegar, or to taste
Salt and pepper, to taste

Doughs & Cakes

BASIC DOUGH FOR RAW-DOUGH PANINI

Yields enough dough for 6 panini (12 rounds)

1 Tbsp + 2 tsp (25 mL) active dry yeast
¾ cup + 1 Tbsp (200 mL) water, lukewarm
2⅓ cups (350 g) all-purpose flour
2 tsp (10 g) kosher salt
1 Tbsp (15 mL) olive oil

Dissolve yeast in water in a bowl. Place about one-third of flour in the bowl of a stand mixer. Add yeast and water and mix briefly with a spoon until ingredients are combined and become a sticky and runny mixture, called a "sponge." Scrape down the sides of the bowl with a rubber spatula and add remaining flour, covering the sponge completely and as evenly as possible. Set the bowl in a warm place, about 80°F (26°C), away from drafts. The sponge is ready when you see large and deep fissures forming in the flour, which usually takes 15 to 20 minutes, depending on the temperature of the room. These fissures mean yeast is active and carbon dioxide is trying to escape through the flour.

Attach a dough hook to the mixer. Add salt to sponge and knead slowly until all ingredients are combined. Increase speed to medium and continue kneading for about 5 minutes. When dough is smooth and shiny, pulls away from the sides, and stretches so thin you could read a newspaper through it, you have developed enough gluten and dough is ready. Add oil to dough and mix until combined. Turn out dough onto a clean, lightly floured surface, cover with a clean cloth, and set in a warm place away from drafts. Allow dough to rest, or "proof," until it doubles in size, or about 30 minutes. Punch down and divide dough into 12 even pieces and roll into round balls. Cover and let rest for another 15 minutes. Roll each into ball into a 4-inch (10 cm) round and proceed as per recipe and the step-by-step instructions on the facing page.

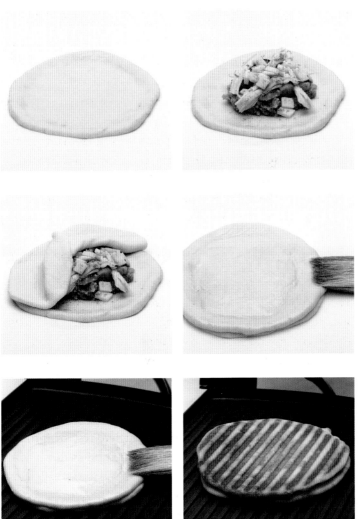

STEP 01: Brush olive oil on edges of dough.

STEP 02: Place filling in center of dough.

STEP 03: Cover filling with another piece of dough and press edges lightly to seal.

STEP 04: Lightly brush top dough with olive oil. Preheat panini press to medium heat (375°F / 190°C).

STEP 05: Place raw-dough panini oiled side down in the panini press.

STEP 06: Lightly brush top side with olive oil and grill for about 5 to 8 minutes, or until bread is cooked and nicely grilled.

CIABATTA

Yields 2 loaves, or 8 buns

SPONGE

⅛ tsp (0.6 mL) active dry yeast

2 Tbsp (30 mL) + ⅓ cup (80 mL) water, lukewarm

1 cup (150 g) bread flour

BREAD DOUGH

½ tsp (2.5 mL) active dry yeast

2 Tbsp (30 mL) milk, lukewarm

2 cups (300 g) bread flour

⅔ cup (180 mL) water, lukewarm

1 Tbsp (15 mL) olive oil

1½ tsp (7.5 g) salt

SPONGE: Dissolve yeast in 2 Tbsp (30 mL) water in a bowl and let stand until mixture is creamy, about 5 minutes. Place flour in the bowl of a stand mixer fitted with a dough hook and add yeast mixture and ⅓ cup (90 mL) water. Knead mixture for 4 minutes, then cover bowl with plastic wrap and let proof, or rest, in the refrigerator for at least 12 hours and up to 1 day.

BREAD DOUGH: Dissolve yeast in milk in a bowl and let stand until mixture is creamy, about 5 minutes. Place flour in the bowl of a stand mixer fitted with a dough hook, add yeast mixture, sponge, water, and oil and knead on low speed until all ingredients are combined, then knead on medium speed for 3 minutes. Add salt and continue kneading for another 4 minutes. (Unlike other bread dough, ciabatta dough is very slack and sticky and full of bubbles.)

Turn out dough into an oiled bowl, cover with plastic wrap and let dough proof for about 1½ hours or until it doubles in size.

Line 2 baking sheets with parchment paper, approximately 12 × 6 inches (30 × 15 cm), and flour well. Turn dough out onto a well-floured surface and cut in half. Transfer each half to a floured parchment sheet and form into irregular ovals approximately 9 inches (22.5 cm) long, or desired shape. Dip your fingers in flour and dimple loaves.

Dust tops of dough with flour, cover with a dampened kitchen towel, and let proof for 1½ to 2 hours, or until almost doubled in size.

At least 45 minutes before you are ready to bake the bread or buns, preheat a pizza stone on lowest oven rack position at 425°F (220°C). Remove towel from dough and slide 1 loaf, along with parchment paper, onto the pizza stone. Bake until pale golden, about 20 minutes. Let loaf cool on a wire rack. Repeat process for second loaf.

SCOTCH PANCAKES

Yields 12–24 pancakes

In a saucepan, heat butter and buttermilk until butter is melted. Remove from heat.

3 Tbsp + 2 tsp (55 g) unsalted butter
2 cups (500 mL) buttermilk
1¾ cups (275 g) all-purpose flour
⅓ cup (75 g) granulated sugar
1 tsp (5 mL) baking soda
1 Tbsp (15 mL) mirin
2 large eggs, beaten

Sift flour into a bowl and pour warm buttermilk mixture overtop, whisking until all the flour is incorporated. Let mixture stand for at least 30 minutes.

In another bowl, whisk sugar, baking soda, mirin, and beaten eggs. Pour egg mixture overtop buttermilk mixture and whisk into a smooth batter.

Heat a nonstick frying pan on medium heat. Spoon about 2 Tbsp (30 mL) batter for each pancake and cook until bubbles form on surface of pancake and edges are dry, then flip and cook the other side. Repeat until all of the batter is used up.

NOTE: You can freeze any extra pancakes.

FRENCH CRÊPES

Yields about forty-eight 3-inch (8 cm) crêpes

1 large egg
2 large egg yolks
¾ cup (185 mL) 2% milk
1 Tbsp + 1 tsp (20 g) granulated sugar
½ cup (80 g) all-purpose flour
3 Tbsp (45 g) unsalted butter

Place egg, egg yolks, and milk in a bowl and whisk until combined. In another bowl, combine sugar and flour, and make a well in the center. Pour egg mixture into well and quickly whisk until thoroughly combined.

Make a brown butter by cooking butter in a heavy saucepan on low heat. When butter starts to foam, milk solids at the bottom of the pan start to turn brown (but are not burnt), and mixture smells nutty, remove from heat. Pour butter over batter and mix well. Allow batter to stand for about 30 minutes.

Heat a nonstick pan on medium heat, remove it from the stove, and pour some batter into the center of the pan. Quickly swirl the pan to make sure batter is evenly and thinly distributed. Return pan to stove and cook crêpe until lightly browned. Flip and cook other side slightly. Slide cooked crêpe onto a plate and repeat process until all batter is cooked.

NOTE: For a different presentation, cook crêpes using the Japanese-style square or rectangular frying pan used to make *tamago* (cooked egg).

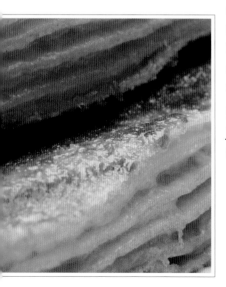

DEVIL'S FOOD CAKE

Yields 2 loaves

Preheat the oven to 350°F (180°C). Line two 8- × 4-inch (20 × 10 cm) loaf pans with parchment paper.

In a bowl, sift the dry ingredients (sugar, flour, cocoa, baking soda, baking powder, and salt) together. Whisk together briefly and make a well in the center. In another bowl, combine all wet ingredients (egg, buttermilk, oil, and vanilla) and whisk together. Pour wet ingredients into dry ingredients and whisk until mixture is smooth and homogenous, but do not overmix.

Divide batter evenly between the 2 loaf pans and bake for 25 to 30 minutes. Invert cakes onto a wire rack and let cool.

1 cup (200 g) granulated sugar
1 cup (150 g) all-purpose flour
⅓ cup + 1 Tbsp (50 g) cocoa powder
1 tsp (5 mL) baking soda
½ tsp (2.5 mL) baking powder
¼ tsp (1.25 mL) salt
1 large egg
1 cup (250 mL) buttermilk
¼ cup (60 mL) peanut oil
½ tsp (2.5 mL) pure vanilla extract

POUND CAKE

Yields 2 loaves

Preheat the oven to 350°F (180°C). Line two 8- × 4-inch (20 × 10 cm) loaf pans with parchment paper.

Sift flour and baking powder together in a bowl and set aside. Using an electric mixer fitted with a whisk attachment, cream butter and sugar until light and fluffy. Add the eggs one at a time, making sure that each one is incorporated before adding the next. Add vanilla extract, incorporating with a rubber spatula. Fold in flour mixture, making sure not to overmix.

Divide mixture between the 2 loaf pans and bake for 50 to 60 minutes. Invert cakes onto a wire rack and let cool.

1⅔ cups (250 g) cake flour
2 tsp (10 mL) baking powder
1 cup (230 g) unsalted butter
1 cup (200 g) granulated sugar
4 large eggs
2 tsp (10 mL) pure vanilla extract

BANANA BREAD

Yields 2 loaves

1¾ cups (270 g) all-purpose flour
1 tsp (5 mL) ground cinnamon
¼ tsp (1.25 mL) salt
1½ tsp (7.5 mL) baking soda
⅓ cup (80 g) unsalted butter
1½ cups (300 g) granulated sugar
2 large eggs
3 ripe bananas, mashed
1 cup (250 g) sour cream
1 tsp (5 mL) pure vanilla extract

Preheat the oven to 300°F (150°C). Line two 8- × 4-inch (20 × 10 cm) loaf pans with parchment paper.

Sift flour, cinnamon, salt, and baking soda together in a bowl and set aside. Using an electric mixer fitted with a whisk attachment, cream butter and sugar until light and fluffy. Add eggs, banana, sour cream, and vanilla, and continue mixing on low speed until ingredients are combined and mixture is smooth and homogenous. Add the dry ingredients and whisk until smooth, but do not overmix.

Divide batter evenly between the 2 loaf pans and bake for approximately 50 to 60 minutes. Invert cakes onto a wire rack and let cool.

SPONGE TOFFEE

Yields about 10 oz (300 g)

Line a 9-inch (22.5 cm) square pan with parchment paper that extends 2 inches (5 cm) beyond the sides of the pan. Have all ingredients measured or weighed and ready to use before you start, as you will need to work very quickly once the sugar is cooked.

Sift together baking soda and flour in a small container. In a large heavy saucepan, combine sugar, corn syrup, and water and bring to a boil on high heat. Without stirring, cook mixture until a candy thermometer registers 320°F (160°C). Once mixture has reached required temperature, remove from heat and whisk in baking soda, flour, and vanilla. Note that the mixture will bubble and rise quite a bit, so be careful not to touch the toffee.

Pour toffee immediately into the prepared pan. Let cool completely. Break into pieces and store at room temperature in an airtight container.

2 tsp (10 mL) baking soda
1 tsp (5 mL) all-purpose flour
1½ cups (300 g) granulated sugar
5 Tbsp (75 g) corn syrup
3 Tbsp (45 mL) water
1 tsp (5 mL) pure vanilla extract

Eggs

TECHNIQUE FOR COOKING EGGS

STEP 01: Prepare all ingredients (eggs, pan with oil, garnish).

STEP 02: Whisk eggs in bowl with fork.

STEP 03: Pour egg into loaf pan and place in preheated 400°F (200°C) oven.

STEP 04: Every minute or so, remove pan and, with a fork, push cooked egg from the pan sides toward the middle. Return pan to oven.

STEP 05: Repeat until almost all the egg is cooked, but center is still slightly runny. Evenly distribute garnish mixture overtop egg. Return pan to oven and continue baking until egg is fully cooked, about 2 to 3 minutes.

STEP 06: Remove egg from the pan, and keep warm.

CHAPTER 8

Pairing Wine & Beer with Panini

Although sandwiches, including panini, do pair well with wines, they also pair very well—better in many cases—with beer. In this chapter, we provide some information pertaining to the pairing of panini with both beverage options. As always, experiment to determine what you like best, and discover for yourself how a well-chosen wine or beer can enhance a well-prepared panino.

PANINI & WINE

You may have noticed that plenty of books have been written on the topic of food and wine pairing. Yet it seems there is not much information available on the pairing of sandwiches and wine—especially panini and wine.

The general consensus when it comes to wines is that the best wines to pair with sandwiches, and panini by association, would be a Beaujolais for red and a dry Riesling for white. One could also follow the guidelines that apply to pairing wine with pizza, since panini are similarly constructed from a meat of some sort (e.g., salami) as well as a cheese and a vegetable garnish or sauce, sometimes just crushed tomatoes. However, there are quite a few factors that one may want to further investigate to select the most appropriate wine for the flavor combination of a specific panino. Following is a list of factors to keep in mind:

BREAD: Depending on the type of bread used for the panino, and the amount of it in proportion to the whole panino, you may consider the wine selection based on the style of bread. For example, a Tuscan-style bread such as ciabatta would pair well with a red wine such as Merlot or Pinot Noir or a white wine such as Chardonnay or Sauvignon Blanc. Keep in mind that some types of bread, such as sourdough, can be tricky. Some experts suggest that sourdough would pair well with the wines indicated for Tuscan bread, yet others claim that these do not pair well at all. The purported reason is that the sourness of the bread changes the pH in one's mouth, causing one to perceive low-acid wines as weak.

CHEESE: Pairing cheese and wine can be difficult because most cheese platters will have several cheeses of different styles and made from different milks. Fortunately, a panino is almost always made with only one cheese and thus one could look at pairing the wine to the cheese, especially when cheese is the main ingredient. Panini made with strong cheeses like roquefort and Gorgonzola are also good candidates for pairing the wine to the cheese, as the cheese will likely be the leading flavor of the panino.

PROTEIN: Where the protein content is predominant in the overall makeup of the panino, again, you may consider the wine selection based on the type of protein. For example, a tuna melt panino, especially with pickled vegetables, would pair well with a young dry white wine. A Beaujolais would work well with a roast beef panino.

SWEET WINE PAIRING: For more information, please refer to these books in the Definitive Kitchen Classics series: *Crème Brûlée* (pages 120–22) for cream-style panini and *Chocolate* (pages 120–24) for chocolate-based panini.

PANINI & BEER

As a rule, we typically prefer matching panini to beers. There are several reasons for this. First of all, wine pairing is typically the domain of upscale, fine-dining restaurants, while panini are typically served in casual dining establishments where specialty beers are more widely available. As a side note, we have noticed specialty beers becoming increasingly available at upscale establishments as more beverage directors, chefs, and even wine lovers come to realize and appreciate that beer has an amazing ability to pair with all kinds of foods. Secondly, more often than not panini are served for lunch rather than dinner, or prepared at home as a quick meal for one or two people. Although two people could conceivably drink a whole bottle of wine over an entire meal, it is less likely for one person over a quick lunch or late-night snack. Beer, on the other hand, is mostly available in smaller bottles, perfect for single servings.

There are those who would suggest that beer is more food-friendly than wine, but we are not quite prepared to agree with that statement. We would, however, certainly agree that beer, more often than not, makes a better pairing choice for panini. This is due in part to the fact that beermaking involves a lot more

ingredients than winemaking. Wine contains only grapes and yeast, but beer can be made from a wider variety of ingredients, including barley (adds sweetness), hops (provides bitterness), and yeast, but also spices, nuts, chocolate, fruits, and even vegetables. As with wine pairing, there are quite a few factors involved with pairing the most appropriate beer to a specific panino. Here is a list of factors to keep in mind:

FLAVOR: As a starting point in wine pairing, we typically suggest to try matching certain flavors in the wine with similar characteristics in the food. And the same approach has equal value when looking at pairing food with beer. For example, you may try a spicy salami panino with a spicy pale ale. As with wine, sometimes contrasting may be a better option to consider. For example, a dry bitter beer with a sweeter panino, like one made with shrimp. Sometimes opposites such as sweet and salty can work wonders. Again, as with wine, keep in mind that beer by itself has its own distinct taste and aroma. A beer will taste different when it is combined with food than it will on its own, as elements in the beer interact with those in the food. This metamorphosis can provide very different taste results; some may be great, while others may not be as positive.

WEIGHT, STYLE & ACIDITY: There is a train of thought that suggests that beer can be categorized much like wine, according to style and weight. For example, lagers would be like white wines, whereas ales would be more like red wines. Light wines such as Sauvignon Blanc and Pinot Noir could be compared to light beers such as lager, Pilsner, and wheat. Medium wines such as Merlot, Zinfandel, or Syrah would be equal to ale, India pale ale, and bock beers. And rich or heavy Cabernet Sauvignon, Malbec, and oak-aged Chardonnay could compare to beers like stout, Chimay, and porter. The bittering acids that hops provide to beer have a similar food-pairing effect as acids do in wines: they cut through the fat or richness of foods. Food for thought! In any event, there are a few distinct differences between the two main style of beers. Ales are typically more fruity and robust whereas lagers are usually crisp and delicate. As with typical wine pairings, the adage that light dishes are best paired with light wines and, conversely, that heavy dishes are best with heavy or rich wines can also apply to beer pairing. For spicy foods and strong or fruity flavors, an ale or wheat beer is typically the best pairing option.

TEXTURE: Just as with sparkling wine and champagne, effervescence in wine or carbonation in beer can cut through fried and fatty foods. Pizza and most panini, for example, can be rich in cheese and sometimes fatty protein like salami. Beer is a perfect match for such foods, particularly ales, Pilsners, or lagers that have enough hoppiness to stand up against the cheese, and good carbonation to cleanse the palate. Keep in mind that a beer that is too warm can taste syrupy, so it is best to serve most beers between 40°F and 50°F (4°C and 10°C).

In the following at-a-glance list you will find beer suggestions based on typical panino flavors. Whether you are considering pairing your panini with a wine or beer, keep in mind that the

first rule of pairing is that there are no rules. Try different types of wines and beers and keep notes; experimentation is the key to finding the best match.

- **WHEAT BEER:** Gruyère / feta / goat cheeses, sweet-fruity Asian flavors, citrus flavors including sweets.

- **STOUT:** Roasted / smoked / barbecued / grilled flavors, salty flavors, stewed / braised flavors, chocolate (best if the beer is the sweeter of the two).

- **PORTER:** Smoked / barbecued flavors, rich / braised flavors such as stew and chili, rich proteins such as sausage / bacon flavors.

- **PILSNER:** Muenster / havarti / Monterey Jack cheeses, seafood like salmon or tuna, Asian / Mexican and spicy flavors.

- **LAGER:** Shellfish, grilled white meats, Indian / Asian / Latin / Mexican and spicy flavors.

- **FRUIT/LAMBIC:** Mascarpone cheese, light white meats, herbs / spices, duck / pork with sweet element such as Peking duck or char siu (avoid with very tart lambic), pickled flavors (especially with tart lambic), sweet fruity flavors.

- **BOCK:** Gruyère / Emmentaler / Swiss cheeses, Cajun flavor, seared flavors including chicken, beef, sausage.

- **ALE:** Burger / steak flavors, Asian / Mexican flavors, spicy / nutty flavors, fried flavors, pizza, cheddar / Parmesan / Romano cheeses.

Look for more information on panini presses and locations where you can purchase them on manufacturers' websites such as Breville (www.breville.com), All-Clad Metalcrafters (www.all-clad.com), De'Longhi (www.delonghi.com), and Cuisinart (www.cuisinart.com). Most of these machines can also be purchased online at Amazon (www.amazon.com), or you can contact or visit stores in your area, including Williams-Sonoma, Sur La Table, and most department stores.

DC DUBY Wild Sweets® Virtual Boutique (www.dcduby.com) features many specialty modern cuisine ingredients including premium commercial-grade high-percentage origin bulk chocolate and other cocoa products. Our website features cooking videos along with panini techniques and tips. We also offer cooking classes in our Wild Sweets Theatre. For more information, to purchase products, or to book a seat in one of our classes, visit the website or call (604) 277-6102.